Leading PROFESSIONAL LEARNING COMMUNITIES

*We are profoundly impressed by the truly heroic performance
of the principals and teacher leaders whom we have met and know who have given
so much of their leadership capacity to create professional learning communities in schools.
Exercising the courage to share authority, decision making, and power is a messy job and not one
for the faint of heart. For it requires not only intellect, but heart and soul as well, to serve as the
concerned and caring individual who brings the professional staff together to address the needs
of students and to commit to learning continuously. This professional learning is conducted with their
school campus colleagues in order to become ever more effective, so that students' successful learning
is promoted and realized. In essence, these school leaders envision the entire school as learning, with
the emphasis first on the professionals whose learning benefits students.*

*We have learned much from these leaders and to them we dedicate this volume with the
sincere hope that it will support and enable other school leaders to restructure their schools,
develop a school culture centered on learning, enhance the performance of staff, and
increase learning results for students.*

Leading PROFESSIONAL LEARNING COMMUNITIES

Voices From Research and Practice

Shirley M. Hord
William A. Sommers
Foreword by Andy Hargreaves

A JOINT PUBLICATION

CORWIN PRESS
A SAGE Company
Thousand Oaks, CA 91320

NATIONAL ASSOCIATION
OF SECONDARY SCHOOL
PRINCIPALS

For information:

Corwin Press
A SAGE Company
2455 Teller Road
Thousand Oaks, California 91320
www.corwinpress.com

SAGE Ltd.
1 Oliver's Yard
55 City Road
London EC1Y 1SP
United Kingdom

SAGE India Pvt. Ltd.
B 1/I 1 Mohan Cooperative
    Industrial Area
Mathura Road, New Delhi 110 044
India

SAGE Asia-Pacific Pte. Ltd.
33 Pekin Street #02-01
Far East Square
Singapore 048763

Printed in the United States of America.

Library of Congress Cataloging-in-Publication Data

Hord, Shirley M.
Leading professional learning communities: voices from research and practice/by Shirley M. Hord and William A. Sommers.
        p. cm.
Includes bibliographical references and index.
ISBN 978-1-4129-4476-2 (cloth)
ISBN 978-1-4129-4477-9 (pbk.)
    1. School improvement programs—United States. 2. Group work in education—United States. 3. Educational change—United States. 4. Educational leadership—United States. I. Sommers, William A. II. Title.

LB2822.82.H667 2008
371.2—dc22   2007026276

This book is printed on acid-free paper.

        08   09   10   11   10   9   8   7   6   5   4   3

Acquisitions Editor:	Dan Alpert
Editorial Assistant:	Tatiana Richards
Production Editor:	Cassandra Margaret Seibel
Copy Editor:	Pam Suwinsky
Typesetter:	C&M Digitals (P) Ltd.
Proofreader:	Charlotte J. Waisner
Indexer:	Terri Corry
Cover Designer:	Rose Storey
Graphic Designer:	Lisa Miller

Contents

Foreword

Professional learning communities are now ubiquitous. Few educational leaders and decreasing numbers of teachers remain unaware of what professional learning communities are meant to be—communities of professionals caring for and working to improve student learning together, by engaging in continuous collective learning of their own. And it is hard not to be convinced by the growing body of evidence that shows when schools and districts with the necessary capacity set about organizing themselves as professional learning communities, and when schools that operate on these principles are compared with counterparts that do not, PLCs have a consistently positive impact on student achievement results.

We are in an age of increasing educational standardization, fear of market competition and administrative intervention, and entrapment in a culture of presentism preoccupied with securing short-term gains in tested achievement results. Professional learning communities offer an optimistic alternative to educators who hang on to loftier learning goals, and to those who believe that professional reflection and collaboration rather than prescription and compliance are still the best ways to achieve them.

This apparent synergy between those who strive for professional renewal and those who insist on immediate achievement gains, coupled with the incontrovertible evidence of the early impact and effectiveness of PLCs, has led to a drive to disseminate PLCs further, to spread them out and scale them up. But beneath and beyond the consensus, professional learning communities are often highly contentious. They can improve student learning or simply elevate scores on high-stakes tests, often at the expense of learning. They can heighten the capacity for community reflection that is at the heart of teacher professionalism, or they can enforce collective compliance with prescribed programs and pacing guides which demean that professionalism. The things that pass for professional learning communities can broaden children's learning, in terms of their curiosity about and mastery of themselves and their world, or they can narrow learning to an almost exclusive focus on literacy, math, and standardized basics. And instead of being sustainable learning communities, PLCs often amount to little more than thrown-together teams performing hurried tasks together. The best writers on, and advocates for, professional learning communities understand these distinctions and take a stand on them. But as Naylor (2005) points out, the worst proponents of PLCs avoid such controversy and stick only to the generalities and technicalities of specifying goals, defining a focus, examining data, and establishing teams—in ways that give no offense to their clients and that do not jeopardize their own commercial prospects.

For these reasons, professional learning communities now need more than passionate and practical advocacy. They also need moral discernment and intelligent critique to distinguish the serious from the superficial, the politically opportune from the authentic and profound. No authors could be better suited to this task than Shirley Hord and Bill Sommers.

Shirley Hord is the originator, the Archimedian source point, of the triple-headed concept, *professional learning community*. Bill Sommers is an experienced administrator and past president of the National Staff Development Council. With their extensive backgrounds in educational evaluation, the implementation of change, and school development, their wealth of insight and experience uniquely equip them to delineate and defend a particular vision of professional learning communities that has educational depth, professional richness, and moral integrity. Thus, their Seven C's for leadership of professional learning communities do not only include the usual advocacy of communication, collaboration, coaching, and change, but they also raise even more challenging issues of *conflict* and how to manage (and not simply eliminate) it, *creativity* in problem-solving, and the sheer *courage* to challenge existing systems when necessary.

But *Leading Professional Learning Communities* is a practical as well as a provocative book. Hord's classic contributions to charting stages of development and awareness in the implementation of change are shrewdly applied to provide instruments that help educators monitor and manage professional learning communities through different stages of development. Sommers draws on his understanding of leadership to show how leaders of professional learning communities need to be initiators rather than merely reactors and managers—since as Machievelli himself understood in *The Prince,* all leadership (rather than mere management) involves opposition and the necessity of dealing with it.

Professional learning communities are paradoxical. They need to focus on the process of learning as well as on measurable results, on long-term transformation as well as on immediate achievement gains, and on being persistent about improvement as well as patient in waiting for the outcome. In its essence, leadership entails working with and indeed thriving on paradox, not merely trying to eliminate or endure it. It is less of a certain science than an imprecise art. To see the development of professional learning communities as nothing more than progression through a series of simple stages or steps, is to reduce the leadership of these communities to simple tasks of management in which groups become teams and learning is equated with test scores. By contrast, being able to grasp the paradoxical nature of PLCs, to acknowledge as well as embrace their pitfalls, and from all this to deepen the learning and raise the achievement standards of all students in the community in question, requires the commitment, courage, and capacity of true educational leadership.

Professional learning communities have already come of age. As you work with your own school or system, this significant book will help you shape and sharpen their maturing identity.

Andy Hargreaves
Thomas More Brennan Chair in Education
Boston College
June 2007

Preface

Welcome to this book, in which we explore and discuss the collective learning that takes place among school professionals in their schools and the role that the principal and other leaders play in the creation and development of this community endeavor. It is abundantly clear that such collegial activities focused on staff learning, cannot happen across the entire school staff without the principal's support and guidance. We have had the opportunity to observe, study, interact, and learn from principals who have changed their schools into settings where the learning of the professionals in the school is valued and supported. The professionals' learning is directly linked to the learning of students, as the school staff takes its learning cues from the needs of students. In these schools, administrators and teachers—in addition to counselors, media specialists, and other professionals—read research and review publications that promise to improve educational practice and apply what they have studied to their own classroom practices.

We emphasize *collegial learning,* for that is the common purpose of the community of professionals who are working to increase their effectiveness. Many descriptions of the professional learning community (PLC) place particular attention on the collaborative work of the community, and this is appropriate, but it is not the whole scenario. As the words of this title and the idea of the book suggest, the focal point is the learning of the professionals done in community. We want to be very clear about this concept of the community learning of professionals, and clarify that the PLC is not just working together on carefully identified tasks but supporting that work through careful study and learning of relevant subject matter. This distinguishes the PLC. And, the principal plays a profound role in participating democratically with the staff so that the learning is determined by the community and always relates to the needs of students.

This book is constructed to provide the principal and other school leaders with readily accessible information that will guide them in preparing to initiate and develop PLCs with their staffs. To that end, we have chosen to organize each chapter into the following parts:

Ticklers. Creating a professional learning community is indeed a journey. To grab the reader's attention, we have set the stage for each chapter by presenting a few comments related to taking a journey or trip to help guide the reader a bit. At the beginning of each chapter we have also included a few quotes from the field, from school-based staff members, and other stakeholders, or literature-derived quotations, from authors who write about organizational learning—all of which are relevant to the particular chapter and foreshadow the content of the chapter.

Rationale. A few paragraphs provide a modest rationale for the importance of the chapter, with questions that give a skeletal outline of the chapter and supply guidance to the reader. These questions can be used by the practitioner as a framework for making professional learning communities a reality in schools.

Major Content. This is by far the largest section and contains the major concepts, themes, descriptions, and explanations of the chapter's content. It is a blend of research and the available literature with practitioner-based observations and behaviors in real schools. This section is the heart and soul or backbone and muscle of the chapter.

Leadership Implications. In this section of the chapter, we draw conclusions about important factors for the leader's consideration and assessment. We cannot emphasize leadership too strongly. We believe that leadership is the glue that holds the organization's vision and practice together, supports the work of the professionals working with students, and can be the catalyst that makes systems work.

Vignette. The vignette is a story or example of a real principal or school leader who exemplifies the theme of the chapter. In these examples we have added a bit of wit and whimsy to lighten the load of the message.

Rocks in the Road. No change is without peril. The rocks are real, and being prepared helps create positive responses to difficult situations. As with any change, know there will be tough issues to face and that they can be dealt with effectively. In this section, we point out barriers, or problems, or issues likely to be encountered and offer suggestions for resolution.

Learning Activities. A few suggestions are given for the reader's consideration in continuing or enhancing their learning about the chapter's content. In some cases, the suggestion is to form a small community (after all, that is what this is all about) to take action for the activity.

Throughout the book, the reader will encounter our theory about the relationship between professional learning and student learning. Figure 1.3 in Chapter 1 depicts this relationship, and the text reinforces it. We are very committed to this idea: Professional development by way of the PLC and other venues nurtures the learning needed by professionals to achieve the desired student learning outcomes.

Chapter 1 articulates the five research-based components of the professional learning community and describes each. In addition, the outcomes that may be expected from implementing the five components are reported for the school staff and for students. Currently, higher education is being asked to give attention to professional learning communities; a brief report of a long-term study of change in pedagogy in a university system stretching across the country of Mexico is shared.

Chapter 2 expounds on the imperative of leadership—the principal's and others' in the school—in the school-based professional learning community, as in any school improvement effort. Chapter highlights include actions to keep the focus on staff learning and hints for continuing conversations about the vision of a learning school.

In *Chapter 3*, the significance of the context wherein a professional learning community is being created and developed is discussed. The impact of the presence, or lack of, structures, such as time and space; policies for when and under what circumstances the community might meet; resources that support the community; and other factors are presented for the principal's consideration. Schedules and structures, routines and regulations all help or hinder the effective functioning of the community.

Chapter 4 responds to the query that many have about getting started and "staying started." Here, different approaches and entries into the existing school organization's way of doing things to introduce a professional learning community are discussed.

Chapter 5 explores the skills needed for operating as a PLC: initiating meaningful conversations with the community; using modes of conversation (dialogue and discussion) for appropriate purposes; supporting staff as they learn to engage in reflective practice; and assisting staff in managing and resolving conflict and using it for enhanced learning.

Chapter 6 focuses on checking progress, measuring or monitoring, or assessing how well the PLC components are functioning; the extent to which the staff's learning in community is being implemented in classrooms; and, finally, what student outcomes result from the PLC's efforts.

The final chapter, *Chapter 7*, looks back and ahead. We reflect on what we have learned ourselves during the work of helping schools, districts, state departments, universities, and others to develop PLCs.

As two people who are continuous learners, we consider also what we have learned as we have worked with each other writing this book. We think it is a good idea to combine two personalities—one concrete/sequential, the other abstract/random—to create a book, but it can be challenging to the individuals. This experience has contributed to our learning, and we share our observations.

We hope you will share in the spirit of community with colleagues so that each of you learns, grows, and changes to become more effective in supporting all students so they may reach high standards of successful learning.

Acknowledgments

We are indebted to Diane, Julie, and Linda, truthful colleagues and clear thinkers who gave careful scrutiny and review of our early drafts of this book. Their observations, confusions, and questions were invaluable in supporting our efforts to make this a reader-friendly and idea-accessible tool for principals, teacher leaders, and others in leadership roles in the school.

Diane Zimmerman is Superintendent of Schools, Old Adobe School District, Petaluma, California. Diane provided her perspective from her experience in leadership roles and her deep knowledge of changing organizations. She developed learning communities as a building principal for many years. She provided the "big picture" of the school district as it relates to professional learning communities in schools.

Linda O'Neal was associate professor at Appalachian State University at Boone, North Carolina, where she provided course work, guidance, and direction to potential principals in the department of educational leadership. She currently serves as executive director of the Southwest Educational Alliance (based in Charlotte, North Carolina), an agency that serves multiple school districts, providing professional learning opportunities for educators. Linda shared with us the concerns, assumptions, and principles of preparing principals for their multifaceted roles and critiqued the manuscript in light of those principles.

Last, Julie Morrow, doctoral candidate and student and practicing principal of the Mooresville Intermediate School in Mooresville Graded School District, Mooresville, North Carolina, provided abundant practical remarks about the text, grounded in the reality of real principals and real schools; her commentary proved to be both positive and reinforcing, and courteously suggested needs for inclusion, expansion, and addition.

To all three, we say, "Million thanks, Colleagues."

While these three helped in multiple ways to guide the development of the text, the Southwest Educational Development Laboratory (SEDL) and its staff stepped in to support the completion of chapters, creation of figures, checking of references, and other important finishing tasks. Nancy Reynolds, SEDL information associate, magician, and amazing librarian, found obscure papers and citations and kept us straight with appropriate attributions. The book also benefits from the contribution of SEDL Web administrator Luis Martinez, a talented graphic designer who transforms concepts and ideas into visual representations, giving life to words. But the person to whom we are the most indebted is Leslie Blair, SEDL communications associate and editor extraordinaire. She took our unclear sentences, awkward statements, and scrambled paragraphs, and made them easy-to-read for our audience.

To these three, we say, "Another million thanks, Colleagues."

Shirley M. Hord and William A. Sommers
May 1, 2007

Publisher's Acknowledgments

Corwin Press gratefully acknowledges the following reviewers:

Diane Payne
High School Principal (retired)
Raleigh, North Carolina

Barb Keating
Principal, K–7
F.W. Howay Elementary School
New Westminster, British Columbia, Canada

Paul Young
Middle and Elementary School Principal (retired)
Lancaster, Ohio

Molly Burger
Principal
Middleton Middle School
Middleton, Idaho

Nadine Rosenzweig
Principal
Valley View Middle School
Pleasant Hill, California

About the Authors

 **Shirley M. Hord,** PhD, is scholar emerita at the Southwest Educational Development Laboratory (SEDL) in Austin, Texas, where she directed the Strategies for Increasing Student Success Program. She continues to monitor the Leadership For Change Project and support applications of the Concerns-Based Adoption Model (CBAM). In addition, she designs and coordinates professional development activities related to educational change, school improvement, and school leadership.

Her early roles as elementary school classroom teacher and university science education faculty at the University of Texas at Austin were followed by her appointment as codirector of Research on the Improvement Process at the Research and Development Center for Teacher Education at the University of Texas at Austin. There she administered and conducted research on school improvement and the role of school leadership in school change. This work focused on the concerns and needs of teachers implementing change in their content knowledge and instructional practices, and how leaders support them through structures and staff development interventions during the change process.

She served as a fellow of the National Center for Effective Schools Research and Development, and was U.S. representative to the Foundation for the International School Improvement Project, an international effort that develops research, training, and policy initiatives to support local school improvement practices. In addition to working with educators at all levels across the United States, Mexico, and Canada, Hord makes presentations and consults in Asia, Europe, Australia, and Africa.

Her current interests focus on qualitative research into understanding and delivering comprehensive educational reform to schools, the functioning and creation of educational organizations as professional learning communities, and the role of leaders, including teacher leaders, who serve such organizations. Dr. Hord is the author of numbers of articles and books, the most recent of which are (with G. E. Hall) *Implementing Change: Patterns, Principles and Potholes* (2nd edition); *Learning Together, Leading Together: Changing Schools Through Professional Learning Communities* (editor); and (with P. Roy) *Moving Staff Development Standards Into Practice: Innovation Configurations.*

 **William A. Sommers**, PhD, of Austin, Texas, is currently a program associate at Southwest Educational Development Laboratory (SEDL). He recently ended a 35-year career in public education as principal of Chaska High School in Chaska, Minnesota. He is a senior fellow for the Urban Leadership Academy at the University of Minnesota and serves on the Board of Trustees for the National Staff Development Council (NSDC). Bill is immediate past president of NSDC.

Bill is the former executive director for secondary curriculum and professional learning for Minneapolis Public Schools. Since 1990, he has been an associate trainer for the Center for Cognitive Coaching based in Denver, Colorado. Bill has coauthored five books, (with R. Payne) *Living on a Tightrope: A Survival Handbook for Principals*; (with D. R. Schumacher) *Becoming a Successful Principal: How to Ride the Wave of Change Without Drowning*; (with J. York-Barr, G. S. Ghere, and J. Montie) *Reflective Practice to Improve Schools*; and (with W. R. Olsen) *A Trainer's Companion*, and *Energizing Staff Development Using Video Clips.*

In addition to writing many articles on the topics of coaching, assessment, and reflective thinking, Bill leads training sessions on poverty, leadership, organizational development, conflict management, brain research, and classroom management. Bill also has served as an adjunct faculty member at Hamline University, the University of St. Thomas, St. Mary's University, the Union Institute, and Capella University.

Imagine . . .

All professionals—teachers, administrators, counselors, media specialists, librarians—in all schools (Grades K–5, 6–8, 9–12) engaged in continuous professional learning. In the professions, such as medicine and law, the membership is expected to review the journals of their field and to attend conferences. They observe each other at their work, offering feedback that leads to increased professional effectiveness. They are expected to examine and explore new methods and approaches to their work as well. Professionals, according to *Webster's*, are characterized by a codified knowledge base, which can be increased consistently through ongoing research that seeks new means by which to expand the effectiveness of its members—professionals maintain familiarity with the research.

Such study of one's profession, especially when done in community with others, where the learning is richer and deeper, has not been the norm of the education community. Educators have typically been isolated physically from others because of the structure of school facilities and the schedules that dominate the school day. This has resulted also in mental isolation, with no colleagues for interaction. However, knowledge is most fruitfully constructed in a social context. Providing the opportunities, the structures and schedules, for school-based educators to come together to learn in community is an important challenge.

School and district staff members understand that the most significant factors that determine whether students learn well are the *competence, caring,* and *commitment* of teachers and administrators. Their expertise, combined with their capacity for communicating and interacting meaningfully with students on their cognitive, intellectual, and emotional levels, results in powerful connections with students that enable them to learn at higher standards of quality and deeper layers of understanding. These educators have a deep commitment to their professionalism and a profound clarity about the purpose of their work. Such schools support their educators in continuous study, reflection, dialogue, and learning.

This book is offered as a means for addressing the challenge of providing for educators' continuous learning and improvement opportunities and increasing their professionalism. One is reminded of Peter Senge's *The Fifth Discipline* (1990), in which he advocates for the learning organization, where "people continually expand their capacity to create the results they truly desire, where new and expansive patterns of thinking are nurtured, where collective aspiration is set free, and where people are continually learning how to learn together" (p. 3).

In many schools, staff learning together is a very new endeavor. Some schools schedule time for grade level or subject matter teams to meet, assuming they are then a professional learning community. The majority of these meetings focus on management, a very legitimate purpose. These meetings are useful and necessary. But they are not typically characterized by professionals meeting together to learn deeper content knowledge, more powerful instructional strategies, or investigating the differentiated and sometimes unique ways that students learn. Unstructured time for human interaction does not assure learning (Kris Hipp, personal communication, January 2007) or productivity to result. The professional learning community label has preceded the concept. As it has spread across the nation, and around the globe, the idea of professional learning community has been translated into a wide array of definitions and descriptions— most of which miss the mark of educators in a school coming together to learn in order to become more effective so that students learn more successfully.

There are research reports, observations of exemplary practice, and good old-fashioned common sense, upon which we draw for this book. Our goal is to translate research-based concepts and exemplary school-based practices into the capacity, or capabilities, of the staff so they support their school in becoming a community of professional learners. The book's intentions are

> To clarify what a professional learning community looks like, acts like, and the results to be gained for staff and students

To recognize the essential and critical role of the principal and other school leaders in working with the school staff to initiate, develop, and maintain an effective professional learning community, and

To offer ideas and suggestions about how leaders may successfully do this work

If these goals are of interest to you, please turn the page.

School reform, redesign, restructuring, and many other "re-_____s" are moving from one education system or school to another across our globe. This implies that new ideas are being implemented and that there is transformation of people, places, and organizations. The simplest word to describe this movement is change.

In many ways change resembles a trip. When going on a trip, the first thing we want to know is, "Where are we going?"

When we ask educators to change, the first question they ask is, "Where are we going?" The next questions include, "Why do you want to go there? What is so good about where you want to go? What's wrong with where we are now?"

In our first chapter, we want to be clear about describing where we are going when we embark on becoming a professional learning community (PLC), why we should go there, and what we expect to find when we arrive. In our experience, education acts much like business that promotes the latest fad, latest new silver bullet, and the newest buzzwords. So, cutting through the chatter and noise of "advertisements" for PLCs, what is this stuff all about?

1

What Is a PLC?

Professional Learning Communities: Definition and Effects

You will not believe this. Our principal and AP invited the whole staff of 34 to participate in conducting a reading class each morning with our students, no matter what our own teaching subject matter is—and we're learning together how to do it. It's really exciting!

Middle school math department chair

Oh, my, I do wish that our school staff worked as a professional learning community like my cousin's in New Jersey. I feel so isolated with no one to talk to or solicit advice about my students' lack of attention in reading time.

Third grade elementary school teacher

Did you see last night's televised school board meeting? The board voted to provide early released time for students on Wednesday so school staffs can meet to learn new strategies for instruction—and this all happened because our principal persuaded other principals to submit a proposal.

Parent of high school student

There are various levels of the hormone TTSP in education. This hormone restricts the belief that change can occur and diminishes the effort put into change projects. TTSP is commonly known as "This Too Shall Pass." Most educators are familiar with it. See if this is true for you. Someone comes up with a new idea, writes a book and several articles, starts presenting workshops, and *voilà!* A star is born. School leaders, wanting to appear up on things, start using the new terminology. Some educators are intrigued and ask questions. Most keep their head down, return to their classrooms, and just ignore the new idea.

This scenario has repeated itself many times. Schlechty (1993), in his model of trailblazers, stay-at-homes, and saboteurs, described change in terms of those people motivated to move with a new challenge and those who resisted the opportunity. Mary Lippitt (2003) explained why frustration, false starts, and sometimes gradual change happen on a regular basis. Seymour Sarason (1990) and Andy Hargreaves and Dean Fink (2006) wrote about the predictable failure of school reform.

We believe, like many other intelligent people, that professional learning communities hold a great deal of promise. We also believe that they will not make an impact if the same old processes of change occur in schools, without the important participation of the principal and other campus leaders. It is with this premise that we attempt to marry research *and* practice to make schools "learningful places" for educators and students through professional learning communities.

It does not require rocket science to notice the pivotal role of the principal in the first and third quotes at the beginning of the chapter. In these two schools, collegial study and learning, positive relationships, and collaborative work are under way or about to be launched. Since the late 1970s and early 1980s, there has been a litany proclaiming the role of principal as gatekeeper or key to change and improvement. Research literature reports widespread agreement about this role of principals (Barth, 1990; Leithwood & Jantzi, 1990; Marzano, Waters, & McNulty, 2005; McLaughlin & Hyle, 2001; McLean & Toler-Robinson, 2001; Rust & Freidus, 2001; Waters & Kingston, 2005). For any who work in schools, whether internally on the staff or externally as consultant or supervisor, it is clear that the role of principal is paramount in any endeavor to change pedagogical practice, adopt new curricula, reshape the school's culture and climate, or take on other improvement targets.

At annual meetings of national, regional, and state associations for elementary and secondary principals, for directors of professional development and coordinators of curriculum and instruction, or for supervisors of bilingual and special education, the hallway topic of conversation is often related to professional learning communities (PLCs). At the intuitive, gut level, the PLC makes good sense. Interestingly, many claim to have a PLC in place at their schools but cannot give a precise explanation of what it is.

The persistent question among those who do not purport to have a PLC in their school is, "How do I get one established?" Although much has been written by researchers and practitioners about the importance of PLCs, staff learning, and collaborative work, there is little solid material for those school reformers who need help creating a PLC in their school. This book responds to this question and to the imperative of the principal's role and that of teacher leaders in the school.

A great deal of courage is required by the principal to make waves, take action for change, and to introduce a new way of doing things. In the early 1500s, Machiavelli (1908/1532) explained in *The Prince*, "There is nothing more difficult to take in hand, more perilous to conduct, or more uncertain in its success than to take the lead in the introduction of a new order of things."

It takes courage to speak up, to be messy with a new way of doing things, to walk the talk. This is not a new state of affairs, as we see from Machiavelli, who lived during the sixteenth century. Such courage requires enormous self-confidence and self-efficacy. Such courage related to establishing a PLC can be supported at the state, district, and local campus levels to give opportunities for principals to exercise their creativity and courage—with responsibility and accountability preserved, of course. But, such courage begins with and can only be developed initially through access to the knowledge base and development of skills necessary for creating a PLC, which is our focus. Thus, this chapter provides the foundation by reporting a review of the research by Hord (2004) and from subsequent studies of PLCs. The research answers several questions:

What is a professional learning community? What does it look like in operation and what are its attributes?

Who are the members of the community of professional learners?

What are the benefits to be derived from working as a learning community of professionals?

The major purpose of this chapter is to describe what effective PLCs look like and do, so that school leaders conjure a mental image of a PLC and use it as a guide when creating a PLC in their schools.

Characteristics of a Professional Learning Community

Interestingly, while the PLC has been touted as a significant and effective school improvement strategy or structure, it has been characterized in endless ways, depending on who defines it. Many administrators proclaim to have a PLC in their school, and many would like to be known for their involvement as a PLC, but the specificity of just what constitutes a PLC has yet to be communicated among many educators. One explanation is that while there has been much talk about the importance of PLCs, little attention has been given to the research studies that have investigated what it is and what outcomes it can produce.

One of this book's authors was queried in the early days of the focus on PLCs, "Does professional learning community mean that you will take the students out into the community for learning activities?" Well, no, was the response, although that is a good idea. Then, the question, "So, does it mean that you will bring professionals in the community into the school to enrich the students' learning?" No, again. These questions suggest that learning about the professional learning community concept and operation is a challenge. So, how can the PLC be described with accuracy and authenticity? Five attributes or components have been gleaned from the literature; they are presented in Figure 1.1.

Shared Beliefs, Values, and Vision

Values and beliefs guide the behavior of individuals no matter where they work or in what endeavor. Therefore, one basic attribute of the PLC is the shared mission and goals that the staff see as their common purpose. How they conceive the purpose of the school, and how they describe their role in accomplishing its purpose frames how they will construct their vision of what the school should look like and how they will work together. In the PLC, the vision grows as people work together over time. The community constructs a shared vision of the improvements that they will work toward for the increased learning of students. A shared vision is a mental image of

Figure 1.1   Components of Professional Learning Communities

Shared Beliefs, Values, and Vision	Shared and Supportive Leadership	Collective Learning and Its Application	Supportive Conditions	Shared Personal Practice
The staff consistently focuses on students' learning, which is strengthened by the staff's own continuous learning—hence, professional learning community.	Administrators and faculty hold shared power and authority for making decisions.	What the community determines to learn and how they will learn it in order to address students' learning needs is the bottom line.	*Structural* factors provide the physical requirements: time, place to meet for community work, resources and policies, etc. to support collaboration. *Relational* factors support the community's human and interpersonal development, openness, truth telling, and focusing on attitudes of respect and caring among the members.	Community members give and receive feedback that supports their individual improvement and that of the organization.

what is important to the organization and its individuals. Such an image should catalyze the individuals to work toward the image in order to realize their vision.

An unrelenting attention to student learning success is the core characteristic of the learning community of professionals (Louis & Kruse, 1995). In the PLC, all are encouraged to participate in creating the vision and to keep it foremost in their minds while planning with colleagues and delivering instruction in the classroom. The vision dictates the parameters of decision making about teaching and learning in the school. As it reflects shared values and beliefs, the vision will focus staff members on how they spend their time, what topics they discuss, and how resources may be distributed.

Not only is the principal involved in creating the vision with the staff, but the principal continuously communicates the vision to all stakeholders, articulating powerful images that foster commitment to the vision by all. This means that throughout the school and its neighborhood community and across the school year, reminders will be posted of what high-quality student achievement and successful student learning look like. Student work can be displayed prominently in the school. Descriptions and examples of high-quality achievement and learning can be shared in the school newsletter, in the region's newspaper, and cryptically on banners, bumper stickers, and on the school's external marquee. The focus is *always* on students and learning. Though each individual in the community is responsible for his or her actions, the common good of the school and its students is considered on a par with individuals' personal ambitions. The individuals become a community whose common purpose is the high-quality learning of all students (Brandt, 1995).

Shared and Supportive Leadership

It is clear, as already stated, that any change in a school must be accepted, appreciated, and nurtured by the principal. In the case of PLCs, accepting, appreciating, and nurturing change may be a difficult challenge for some principals, because one of the defining characteristics of PLCs is that power, authority, and decision making are shared and encouraged. The PLC structure in a school is one of continuous adult learning, strong collaboration, democratic participation, and consensus about the school environment and culture and how to attain that. The sharing of power and authority may be tough not only for the principal, but for the staff as well. Historically, teachers have been acculturated to see the principal as all-powerful, all-wise, and all-competent. It is difficult for teachers to propose new ways of thinking and doing when the principal is viewed in such a way. Administrators as well as teachers must be learners, who together are openly discussing instructional problems and exploring solutions to the problems that they identify. But also, it is important to realize, as Hargreaves and Fink (2006) noted, "The principal is not made irrelevant by the positively distributed leadership that professional learning communities represent" (p. 127).

Kleine-Kracht (1993) put it well by stating that in a PLC no longer do "teachers teach, students learn, and administrators manage. . . . [There is] the need for everyone to contribute" (p. 393). The contribution is based on sharing decision making with all professionals in the school, realizing that there are boundaries that reserve some decisions for the singular attention of the principal. This means that the boundaries should be determined and shared early on so that the staff understands the parameters within which they can make decisions.

It also means that a culture of collegiality must be developed over time. In a recent article, Roland Barth (2006) described and distinguished such a culture by the following actions of educators (p. 11):

- Talking with one another about their practice
- Sharing their craft knowledge
- Observing one another while they are engaged in their practice
- Rooting for one another's success

Intrator and Kunzman (2006) suggest that turning the typical competitive culture of traditional schools into one of collegiality should start "with the soul" of staff, asking them to be introspective and to articulate a coherent personal vision of teaching and learning. This can be initiated by the principal asking each staff member to write two or three sentences indicating his or her purpose for being on the staff in the school. Asking them to share in small groups of three, they will then craft a summary statement. Integrating these three declarations into one easy-to-understand, crisp paragraph results in expressions of the school's mission. Being able to articulate their philosophy and ideas contributes to the staff's development of leadership as well as vision creation.

This brings us back to the attribute already noted about vision and indicates the interrelatedness of the five attributes. Most students of school improvement will agree that transforming a school's culture to one of collegiality is a large and difficult challenge for principals.

They must model the concept themselves with their teachers (and with other principals). Please note the last implementation strategy in the "Leadership Implications" section later in this chapter.

Collective Learning and Its Application

A PLC in schools and other organizations is demonstrated by the staff—from *all* assignments as administrators and teachers, and from all grade levels and departments (in schools), and from all levels of the organization and divisions (in other organizations)—coming together to study collegially and work collaboratively. They are continuously learning together and applying what they have learned to their work. The major emphasis is on collective learning, when individuals learn more than if they are learning independently. The PLC is not just about collaboration; it is collaborating to learn together about a topic the community deems important.

Note that the entire staff is involved in the community of learning, and the learning is focused on more effective teaching and increased student learning. One is reminded of a story told by Roland Barth (personal communication, no date). He tells of entering a school and looking to find the principal. Lacking success, he stopped a youngster in the hallway and inquired about where to find the principal.

"Through that door," the student said.

The sign above the door read: "Al Jones, Head Learner." All the professionals in this school were involved together in learning. Successful learning communities build shared knowledge bases, and this knowledge contributes to enhanced possibilities for the community's vision.

The learning in successful learning communities is based on collegial inquiry and on reflection by the participants and their dialogue about their reflection. The staff conducts conversations about instruction and students and teaching and learning. These conversations can be initiated by the principal asking the staff questions about the student data they are studying, about which areas students have achieved well and not so well, and about where the staff should place attention for instruction. The staff members apply their concerns to problem solving and create new conditions for learning for students. Such new conditions could be new instructional strategies for challenged learners, new curriculum, revising regulations and policies to better serve students, and so on. The significant factor here is that the learning and reflection of the professionals is continuous and focuses on students and their benefits. We recall a story about the first faculty meeting of a principal who was hired "to turn the high school around." His first greeting, advanced in a calm and warm manner was, "This year the conversation will be about students and instruction"—period.

Keeping the conversation about students and instruction at a high-quality level is a clear mandate for the principal who is joined by other staff members as they participate democratically and develop their expertise in this activity. The conversation and learning is ultimately initiated by staff investigating student performance data to ascertain where students have accomplished well and where keener attention needs to be given. Identifying student needs and areas for attention indicate to the staff where they need to learn new content or instructional strategies so that they become more effective teachers and administrators. After they determine what they need to learn, they then explore how they will learn: from someone on staff, from a central office specialist, from a colleague in another school, from an external consultant. In a word, the learning is embedded in the everyday work of the staff.

After their learning, the principal and other leaders challenge the teaching staff to plan how they will collaborate to incorporate their new learning into their teaching plans and activities or into their building-level administrative practices. Guided by the principal or teacher leaders, the staff develops a model plan to guide their transfer of their newly gained knowledge and skills to their classrooms. After their initial efforts at implementing their learning, they debrief to determine if or how they should revise, strengthen, change or continue their new approach. Who leads this? A growing array of leaders on the staff, who are developing their leadership skills. This cycle of reflection, learning, and assessment of effects is continuous. It provides the monitoring so necessary for new practices to be implemented well and for the entire staff to be aware of the effects of their new practices.

Supportive Conditions

The research on professional learning communities informs us about the logistics of PLC—the when, where, what, and how the staff regularly and frequently come together as one group to do their reflection, inquiry and learning, problem solving and decision making, the work that characterizes the purpose of the PLC. There are, however, two types of supportive conditions: the logistical conditions noted previously and the capacities and relationships developed across the participants in order that they work well and productively, and pleasantly, with each other.

Physical and Structural Factors

One of the most challenging factors schools face in initiating and creating a PLC is that of time. However, time is a factor that central office, superintendents, and school boards can influence. That is, they can promote the value of a PLC by providing time for school staffs to meet within the instructional day. Districts have found a way to do this by extending the instructional day by 20 minutes four days a week, and abbreviating it on the fifth day when students are released early so that staff may meet as a group for conversation and learning. A variety of other ways to gain time for staff to meet have been proposed by various individuals, but most result in small amounts of time in which little substantive work can be accomplished, or the frequency and regularity of meetings are missing.

Boyd (1992) enumerated a list of physical factors needed in a context conducive to change and improvement: availability of needed resources; schedules and structures that reduce isolation; and policies that provide greater autonomy, foster collaboration, provide effective communication, and provide for staff development. Louis and Kruse (1995) offer a similar list: time to meet and talk, physical proximity of the staff to one another, teaching roles that are interdependent, communication structures, school autonomy, and teacher empowerment.

Related to the challenges of time and space, it may be necessary for large school staffs (those that exceed 30–35 members) to form smaller groups to meet for learning together.

Relational Factors and Human Capacities

Bringing together individuals who do not respect or trust each other is problematic. The work of Bryk and Schneider (2002), who reanalyzed the large amount of data collected in the Chicago schools restructuring project, brings us excellent information about trust building and its significance for a staff learning together and making decisions about actions to take. Trust provides the basis for giving and accepting feedback in order to work toward improvement. Building trust is a goal requiring substantial time and activities provided to individuals that enable them to experience the trustworthiness of colleagues and for the individual to extend or become trustworthy to complete the cycle.

Principals can contribute to the collegial attitudes and relationships demanded of school staff by nurturing the human capacities
demanded of PLC work. They do this by helping staff relate to one
another, providing social activities for staff members to get to know
each other on a personal level (think ice cream socials here, or volley-
ball games after school in the school gym, or potluck suppers once in a
while where staff gather to eat and socialize), and creating a caring
environment. An example of this last item is the principal who released
a teacher from instructional responsibilities so that the teacher could
take an ailing parent to the doctor (the principal "subs" for the teacher).

Shared Personal Practice

The review of a teacher's practice and instructional behaviors by
colleagues should be the norm. This is not an evaluative process, but
part of peers helping peers that includes teachers visiting each other's
classrooms on a regular basis to observe, take notes, and discuss their
observations with the teacher they have visited. In this way, teachers
facilitate the work of changing practice with each other. They support
the implementation of new practices through peer coaching and feedback. This process is grounded in individual and community improvement, but can only be done meaningfully if there is mutual respect
and trust among the members of the staff. This dimension of PLCs is
likely to be the last to be developed because of the history of isolation
most teachers have experienced.

Visiting, observing, and giving feedback are learned skills. School
leaders could conduct professional development to teach these skills,
or, most assuredly, they could be taught by central office. A first step
in implementing peers-helping-peers could be initiated with the
whole school learning together some new strategy, such as questioning, for example. This design means that all staff learn the questioning strategies, practice them in their classrooms, then pair up and
visit each other to give feedback. Central office could support this
process by providing subs to serve in the visiting teacher's classroom
while she or he is observing a colleague.

Teachers find help, support, and trust as a result of the development of warm relationships with one another. But the principal facil-
itates these relationships. When these positive relationships develop,
Wignall (1992) suggests that "teachers . . . are comfortable sharing
both their successes and their failures. They praise and recognize one
another's triumphs, and offer empathy and support for each other's
troubles" (p. 18).

As a principal, Barth (2006) noted that he had tried various means by which to entice teachers to observe each other and give feedback, to no success. Finally, one teacher asked in a faculty meeting, "Well, Roland, when was the last time we saw another principal observing you?" This encouraged Principal Roland to invite another principal to observe him in a faculty meeting and to give him feedback. In turn, Barth visited his colleague, observing and giving feedback. This set of actions provided the impetus for the teachers to engage in peer visitation and feedback—the logjam was broken.

On a personal note, one of this book's authors moved from elementary classroom teaching to serve on the staff at a research center to study the change process in schools and universities. Not knowing what to label the phenomenon, I was dumbfounded by the way the research staff and its director interacted. The staff of 18–20 professionals met with great frequency and high intensity around a very large library table. I was immediately impressed by the fact that the director did not sit at the head of the table, but along the side. I was equally impressed by the discussion of ideas and learning assignments staff gave themselves.

The expectation was that all would be involved in studying the knowledge base on identified factors impacting the change process in schools, learn with and from each other, and make collegial decisions about where to focus the research. Having moved from a context where I was told what to do to a culture of thinking and learning, collaborative problem solving, and demonstrating leadership made for a steep learning curve. Being in this culture changed my life from being a marshmallow to being a Wizard of Oz—crafting ideas, supporting them, and influencing others of their value.

The experience changed my life. It allowed—encouraged—my growth and development through learning with others. I developed confidence and gained personal valuing of my own capacity to make a contribution to our work, and subsequently, to the profession. I had become a professional! It was after several years of this experience that I learned I had become a member of a community of professional learners.

Membership in the Community of Professional Learners

We have chosen to focus on the school *campus professionals*, who have the most direct influence on student learning. These participants have the responsibility and accountability to deliver an effective instructional program to students so that all students learn well. It is incumbent on these educators to continuously study the literature and research reports to become informed about the latest and most influential teaching and learning strategies available so that their performance continues to be enhanced by their learning. To continue to increase student achievement, these educators change their practices to benefit students. Change is learning: it's as simple and complicated as that (Hord, 2000b). The learning begins with the educators.

Many schools make it possible to schedule common conference and planning periods for grade-level teachers in the elementary school and academic subject discipline teachers in the secondary school so they can meet in professional learning teams. Clearly, this is an important structure so that faculty members have the opportunity to address the particular needs of the students for whom they have primary responsibility. However, in addition to the small teams, it is imperative that the whole school staff—administrators and teachers—meet regularly and frequently as a whole school community (at least once a month; twice a month is a much better arrangement) to address schoolwide goals and the staff's learning. These regular all-staff meetings will make it possible for the staff to become increasingly effective so that all students are successful learners (more about this in Chapter 3).

District office staff, parents, business partners, community social service agencies, policymakers at the various levels all have impact on schools. They provide parameters and boundaries, regulations and mandates, and shape what the school curriculum and instruction, and teaching and learning expectations may be. But the most significant factor in whether students learn well is found in their interactions with the educators in the school. Therefore, the school professionals constitute the membership of the PLC. By this we mean *all* educators are convened in the community (see Figure 1.2). This does not deny the importance and utility of teachers meeting in grade-level and department teams. This is an important activity so that teachers focus on the specific needs of their particular students. But, so that the entire staff shares a common vision, learns collectively, and collaborates in working toward that vision, the total school professional community meets regularly and frequently to learn together.

One could imagine each of the grade-level or department teams as a ship in a fleet or convoy. Each ship is solving its own issues and

Figure 1.2   Professional Learning Community Membership

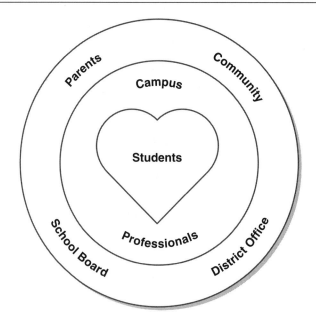

SOURCE: *From Achieving Learning Success for Each Student: Transforming Intentions Into Reality* by Northwest Regional Educational Library for the Association Partnership including AASA, NAESP, and NASSP. Used with permission of Northwest Regional Educational Laboratory, Portland, OR.

problems that arise, but they are all going in the same direction in order to arrive at a mutually decided destination. Without this *whole school professional learning, involvement, and collaboration,* one does not have a professional learning community in the school.

Professional Learning Community Benefits

Although to date there is only a small body of research that has explored professional learning communities, the reports have been clear about the effects or results of school staffs working as PLCs. These benefits accrue to both staff and to students in various settings. A review of this literature (Hord, 2004) informs us about these outcomes.

Staff Results

When staff members work together as a PLC, the typical isolation experienced by teachers and administrators is reduced. When the staff members come together to hold conversations about teaching and learning, the participants demonstrate higher commitment to the goals, mission, and vision of the school. Their energy and enthusiasm contribute to a higher probability that the vision of the school will be realized. Together the staff members engage in powerful learning that adds to their knowledge base and repertoire of technical skills that increases their effectiveness. In addition, staff gain deeper understanding and meaning related to their content area and to the curriculum. They gain an appreciation for the vertical articulation of skills and competencies expected of students across the grades. This contributes to educators' exercising their roles in helping all students meet expectations for reaching high standards of learning.

The development of all students in all subjects is explored and a collective responsibility for all students' successful learning is manifested. Teachers observe and adapt their teaching approaches to meet the needs of all students, and they do this more thoroughly and systematically than do teachers in traditionally organized schools. Teachers in PLC schools exhibit higher morale as they support each other, absences are reduced, and teachers feel renewed and inspired professionally.

A recent study by Gonzalez, Resta, and De Hoyos (2005) focused on faculty in higher education as they implemented new classroom practices. A constructivist approach to teaching and learning was handed down to the faculty but was supported by abundant professional development and other facilitators over a three- to five-year period. A factor in the support was the encouragement to organize faculty into professional learning communities. This project of a university system that constitutes 33 campuses spread across the country of Mexico was assuredly a significant systemic change. One interesting finding was that those faculty who viewed themselves as part of a PLC expressed concerns about their *impact on students.* Those faculty who did not perceive themselves as belonging to a PLC expressed concerns about *managing their classrooms* and other logistical issues such as managing materials, time, and their syllabi.

In order to reach the desired student learning outcomes, we "backward map" (see Figure 1.3). We identify the desired learning outcomes for students (1) and then consider staff learning (2), which precedes student learning (1). In the PLC, staff give attention to professional learning and development (3) that will support what they need to learn in order to prepare themselves to work more effectively for students. Factors in the system (4) contribute to this theory of change by providing resources, leadership, policies, a culture of continuous improvement, and others.

Figure 1.3   Theory of Change: The Relationship Between Professional
Learning and Student Learning

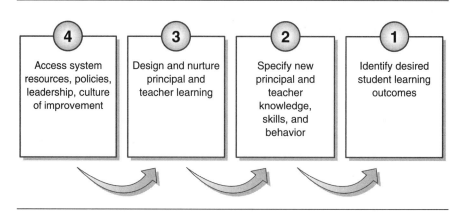

Staff who are involved in a PLC provide higher intellectual learning tasks for their students. The bottom line of the PLC is staff learning in order to increase student learning. Hence the importance of the staff learning in community, which is more powerful than independent learning. PLC staff use this graphic to guide their work, and the staff are guided by school leaders who supply student data for identifying student needs as the starting point.

Student Outcomes

Lee, Smith, and Croninger (1995) reported important student results when their study teachers and administrators worked as a PLC. In these schools, students accomplished greater academic gains than students in traditional schools. These gains were achieved in reading, math, science, and history. Smaller achievement gaps were found between students from different family backgrounds (socio-economic status, ethnicity, language, culture) when the staff operated as a PLC. Students and staff related more meaningfully with each other, resulting in fewer students cutting classes and a decline in the dropout rate.

In a state-level study, Bobbett, Ellett, Teddlie, Olivier, and Rugutt (2002) observed strong positive relationships between the school performance of the students and teachers who were part of a positive professional culture in the school. The researchers controlled statistically for the effects of poverty and found that teachers' professional commitment and collegial learning and teaching in the school accounted for 23 percent of the variation in school effectiveness and student outcomes on the state's achievement test.

More studies are needed that trace the academic outcomes of students in schools where the staff members are organized and work as a professional learning community. A recent publication that sheds such light is that by McLaughlin and Talbert (2006) who investigate professional strategies that improve student achievement.

Leadership Implications

The school principal is often the catalyst for launching a PLC, and for the staff's development into a way of working collaboratively, sharing expertise, wisdom, and craft knowledge with colleagues. This is not the typical way that schools are organized or how they do their work. The typical school functions as a bee-hive, with each worker in his or her own cell with little interaction with neighbors, except to leave to forage for food, and to mate with the queen (a duty relegated to a few). How then can leaders break the cell walls and foster professional interaction among staff rather than continuing to permit the whining about Johnny's inability to read well or Suzie's mother who can't seem to get her child to complete her home assignments.

Implementation Strategies

Change process research informs us about introducing new practices into schools. Six strategies have been identified (Hall & Hord, 2006) that must be exercised if change is to be implemented well. They are presented here in abbreviated form. For more information, insight, and understanding, see Chapter 9 in Hall and Hord (2006).

The first strategy is *articulating a shared vision.* In this activity, the principal invites staff to engage in conversation about the new practice (in this case, PLC) and discuss why it could be useful to the school or how it will fill some agreed-upon need. There are various other ways to introduce a new practice or new facet of the environment so that staff members are more ready to accept it: inviting staff from a PLC school to report their work and its results, taking staff to another school to see its PLC in action, reviewing videotapes that reveal how teachers engage in PLC. At this point in this chapter, suffice it to say that a clear description of the new idea must be developed collaboratively with all who will be involved so that a shared vision, or mental image as it will appear in action, is created.

The second strategy uses the vision of change—that is, PLC—to *develop a plan* that will engage the staff in realizing the vision. Resources that will be required are specified at this point.

The third strategy is the investment in and *provision of professional development* so that participants gain the knowledge and skills to be able to "do" the new work, to perform as a PLC.

The fourth strategy, *checking progress,* is needed to determine if the participants are "getting it" and are able to implement the new practice(s) and are developing as a PLC. Well-organized and -delivered professional development to a large number of people is the starting point of learning how to use new skills needed for acting as a PLC. Assessing the progress of individuals in learning the new ways or skills and applying them appropriately is necessary in order to follow through with the next strategy.

The fifth strategy, *providing assistance,* is delivered to individuals and is based on the assessment of each individual's progress as noted in the previous strategy.

The overarching and sixth strategy, serving as an umbrella over all the strategies, is the culture or *context for change.* Much currently has been written about school culture so that we are more fully informed about the factors necessary for supporting staff in the change process. Risk taking comes to mind, as does trust. We believe the PLC context is the most powerful context for supporting staff's learning and increased effectiveness, and, thus, improved student achievement.

Principal's Personal Behaviors

The six factors just noted are focused on strategies that will contribute to the probability that a new concept, program, practice (or even a new person), or PLC, will be introduced and implemented successfully so that the promises it purports are achieved. Terry Deal and Kent Peterson (1990) share ways that principals act personally, taking on behaviors such as modeling what the new practice or innovation involves. In the early part of this chapter, we mentioned Roland Barth taking on the behavior of inviting colleagues to observe him and give him feedback. It was only at this point that the staff were convinced to do likewise. There are other behaviors, of course, and they are the topic of another chapter.

Vignette

Cottonwood Creek School: Principal's Role, Staff Impact, Student Outcomes

In the early research studies of PLC conducted by staff of the Southwest Educational Development Laboratory (SEDL), a great deal of exploration finally uncovered one school in each state of SEDL's five-state region. In Texas, we found Cottonwood Creek School (Hord & Rutherford, 1998) and interviewed the current principal, former principal, and multiple teachers. The Cottonwood Creek story is characterized strongly by the principal leadership factor and its effect on the PLC in the school. A brief account of this story follows.

Cottonwood Creek School was built in the 1920s in what is now a large urban city in the Southwest. Its student population was and remains predominantly Hispanic, and families are in the lower socioeconomic strata. In a 10-year period before it developed as a PLC, Cottonwood had seen a succession of three principals. The first was a laissez-faire administrator who did little to disrupt the way the school and its educators were operating, an approach that could be characterized as "Ho-hum, so what's new?" The second principal initiated strategies to improve the professional culture of the school's staff and was making progress but was succeeded by the third administrator, who sabotaged his predecessor's efforts. The term of this administrator resulted in a school torn by tension, strife, and ill feelings. Student scores moved from bad to worse, and teachers were unhappy with their students and their school.

A new principal, who judged the healing of teachers and staff to be a high priority, came to the school with ideas about how to engage the staff in collegial learning and interaction, and collaborative and supportive work that would transform the school. At the point of the new principal's entrance, students scored in the lowest quartile of schools in this large district. Five years later, with the principal's support and guidance, and when the educators' professional learning and collegial work (PLC) was fully flourishing, the students had moved to the top quartile of the district's elementary schools.

At this point, a new principal came who gave no attention to supporting the staff's activities that would permit them to continue to learn and work together. Without structures and schedules to provide time and place for their work, the PLC gradually faded into oblivion. What happened to student scores? They, too, faded. This story points to two important lessons: the relationship between teachers' learning and students' learning, and the significance of the principal in the endeavor.

Rocks in the Road

Bringing individuals who have worked singly into community is an issue. One of the components of PLCs suggests that identifying the beliefs that the staff shares about the mission or purpose of the school is foundational. Developing a clear and shared understanding of the school's purpose across the entire staff provides the basis for encouraging and persuading staff in continuous and collegial learning in order to serve students well—this is true if the staff articulates that their purpose is to serve students through effective instructional content and practices. Pointing to the mission and challenging staff to define a vision of the staff at work when it is accomplishing this mission should certainly include the idea of continuous and intentional staff learning, so that staff always are increasing their effectiveness, leading to students' increased successful learning.

There is, of course, the issue of "We've always done it *this* way. Why do we have to change?" As Machiavelli noted in the 1500s, it is a challenge to move people from their comfortable and accustomed routines and behaviors. If this situation is not a rock in the road, it is certainly a thick layer of small stones or very grainy gravel. A means for smoothing the road on this issue is to focus participants on student benefits and the mission of the school, which should point uppermost to the well-being and successful learning of all students. Use data here. Engage staff in reviewing data, understanding it, interpreting it. Ask, "What do the data tell us about our students? What do they need? What do we need to change in our work to serve them better? What will we need to learn to do that?"

Engage in Learning Activities

Form a dyad or triad of colleagues to serve as a PLC and do the following activities:

1. What does the PLC in your school "look" like in operation? To answer this question, solicit information from the staff. For example, use the five attributes of a PLC to make a protocol—a list of questions—for collecting data. Arrange to interview one teacher in the school at each of the different grade levels, or in different departments, using the protocol. Principals could collect data in a school other than their own and ask that school's principal to collect data in the first principal's school. In other words, they serve as collectors of data in each

other's schools, but not in their own. Aggregate the data to make a picture of your school as a PLC based on this small sample.

Now, do Activities 2, 3, and 4:

2. Interview the principal(s) at the school, using the protocol as with the teachers. Compare the principals' interview results with that of the teachers.

3. Share the report (the result of Activities 1 and 2) with the principal(s), asking them to verify the report and to give examples of what each did to reach the results indicated in the report. If they deny the results, ask them to describe the PLC in the school using the protocol.

4. Review the data with other school leaders in your school to find weak attributes indicated by the data, and consider how to work to strengthen these.

Now that we know where and why we are going some place, we want to know, "Who is arranging this trip? Do they know what they are talking about?" More important, "Who is taking the lead in planning the trip? Where we will go? And how much will it cost?" Sometimes we leave the details to a travel agent, but from our experience, we want more input into the planning rather than just letting someone else decide what we want.

So, who will lead? If they lead, will others follow? How do you get consensus on what to visit, how much time to invest, and how we will make decisions once we get in the middle of the trip of change?

To make a productive and pleasant trip, we have to have agreement on where we will go and what specific areas we will visit. The leaders will guide us in creating a shared vision of what we want; this is critical, and it takes everyone to contribute. How do we distribute the leadership roles and responsibilities on this trip? What are some of the strategies that seem to work, to include rather than exclude? Are there specific ways to organize to maximize our talents and minimize our costs?

2

Why Leadership?

Leadership Imperatives for Professional Learning Communities

Leadership is action not position.

Donald McGannon

The leader has two jobs: (1) to be the lead learner, and (2) to develop other leaders.

Noel Tichy

A school can fulfill no higher purpose than to teach all its members that they can make what they believe in happen and to encourage them to contribute to and benefit from the leadership of others.

Roland Barth

As we discussed in Chapter 1, the roles and behaviors of the principal are critical elements in how a school operates as a professional learning community (PLC). For years the literature and research have been replete with quotes about leadership, its influence on school climate, and its results on student achievement. Principals, specifically, are the lynchpins of school change, providing the necessary modeling and support required for a learning school. We agree that leaders make a difference. They make a difference through their leadership capacity to affect the system around them and on the future of the organization. We want to state that leadership teams and teacher leaders, both formal and informal, are critical in moving the school into professional learning communities.

Fullan (2001) advised, "The role of leadership is to 'cause' greater capacity in the organization in order to get better results" (p. 65). We suggest that there are specific strategies and actions the principal must take, but in the final analysis, student outcomes will indicate whether or not leaders and their schools are successful.

In one urban high school, the principal trained 13 teachers in Adaptive Schools (Garmston & Wellman, 1999). Included in the training were skill sets of facilitation, running effective meetings, and strategies to focus conversations using dialogue. At the beginning of the following school year, these teacher leaders started facilitating each others' departments. For example, the physical education teacher was the facilitator of the world language department. The department chair was able to become part of the department instead of trying to facilitate, represent her own language area, and be a colleague all at the same time. The outside facilitator could keep the focus on the agenda, ask clarifying questions without threat, and remain less emotionally involved in difficult issues. Outside facilitators could ask the hard questions about data, student learning, and collegial learning, which proved to make meetings more meaningful and efficient.

In *Building Leadership Capacity in Schools*, Linda Lambert (1998) begins to make the connection of leaders and leadership:

> School leadership needs to be a broad concept that is separated from person, role, and a discreet set of individual behaviors. It needs to be embedded in the school community as a whole. Such a broadening of the concept of leadership suggests shared responsibility for a shared purpose of community. (p. 5)

Yes, we need leaders and they have a specific role, but as Lambert suggests, at the same time we need to develop leadership throughout the school, sharing the responsibility for learning and sharing decision making where possible. Farson (1996) notes that we need leadership, not leaders. It is obvious to those of us who work in schools, like Tichy's quote at the beginning of this chapter; we need leadership at all levels. Developing sustainable leadership to keep the focus on staff and student learning across the school is a difficult task. Developing professional learning communities creates ongoing conversations, encourages participation, and sharing of educators' learning. These must be part of the principal's leadership role and responsibilities.

The central task of the leader is to involve others in creating a shared vision for the organization. "Over the last few decades, as our knowledge of leadership in general and our understanding of school administration in particular have deepened, we have learned that it is more helpful to scaffold school administration on broader concepts of leadership" (Murphy, 2006, p. 51). The principal, more than any other position in the school, identifies, models, and brings the policies and procedures to life. The principal's actions, not just his or her words, make believers out of teachers. And beyond the principal's actions, it takes the actions of the teacher leaders to create inclusive leadership.

When the principal and staff members focus on their own learning, together they begin to develop ways to make learning happen. It is not enough to say we believe in staff learning, we have to demonstrate that by meeting, learning together, sharing knowledge and skills. Again, collegial learning—not just the words—creates professional learning communities. When the principal sustains focus on staff learning, student learning increases. Teachers who function at higher cognitive levels produce students who function at higher cognitive levels. If the conversations in schools continue to be organized around learning, this sends a message to everyone that the driving vision for what we do is learning.

In recent work done at Mid-continent Research for Education and Learning (McREL), Marzano, Waters, and McNulty (2005) quote Leithwood, Seashore-Louis, Anderson, and Wahlstrom (2004), stating that next to teacher quality, leadership and school culture have the most effect relative to student learning. Leadership is fast becoming a high-leverage, high-focused part of student achievement. Fullan and Hargreaves (1996) describe principals who establish shared leadership and supportive organizational structures that encourage teachers to take responsibility as having greater success in achieving school improvement goals than when they neglect these strategies.

Art Costa asked a principal 20 years ago, "What are you doing to make your school a more mentally stimulating environment for staff?" In other words, he asked how the principal was initiating and encouraging the staff to work on learning as a community rather than working in their rooms as individual teachers. The principal responded, "You mean I have to do that, too?" Dr. Costa went on to say that if staff were not in a mentally stimulating environment, there is no reason we should believe they would create such an environment for their students. These comments were foreshadowing the need for professionals to work together sharing their collective wisdom throughout the staff. However, now the research supports that idea from years ago. We believe it will continue to be a fundamental question as we create learning cultures for our staffs and students.

As the quote at the beginning of the chapter says, leaders have two jobs: first, to be the head learner, and second, to develop other leaders (Tichy, 1997). Being the head learner is tantamount to modeling learning. The principal does not have to be, nor should she or he be, the top content specialist. However, the principal leads primarily by modeling. How do we model learning? How do we act as a learner and develop other leaders at the same time we keep the school running? We believe most of us who went into school administration wanted to make a larger impact on student growth and development. We probably remember thinking, "Now I can be an instructional leader." As we talk to thousands of principals, however, the mundane drives out the important.

The saying, "Things that matter most should never be at the mercy of things that matter least" has been attributed to philosopher and dramatist Johann Wolfgang von Goethe. Several questions arise from that statement and drive our discussion in Chapter 2:

> Why should a principal and other leaders keep the focus on staff learning and not get bogged down in the day-to-day administrivia?

> Why maintain focus on learning?

> What is the role of the principal in facilitating professional development and creating professional learning communities?

We address the *why* of leadership in this chapter. Without knowing why, people get confused or lose interest. As many have said, If you know *why*, you can survive the *what*. We know it is important to be able to answer the question of, "Why do this?"

Vision: What Are We Trying to Do?

In Chapter 1 we talked about how important it is for the staff and school to have a clear vision and to keep it consistently in focus.

Although leadership and organizational literature emphasizes the critical element of having a shared vision, developing a shared vision and keeping the focus on that vision is no easy task. So, how do we develop, implement, and sustain a clear shared vision for the organization? One way is to talk about it. Economist Ernesto Gore proclaimed, "Organizations are made of conversations" (as cited in Perkins, 2003, p. 17). Our question is, "What kinds of conversations are taking place in your teams, sites, and organization?"

Another perspective comes from Spillane (2006) in his book *Distributed Leadership*. Leadership in schools requires a network of formal and informal leaders working together for common goals. The interactions between formal and informal leaders are indicative of collaboration and a focus on learning. The strength of the interactions between the leaders and the followers are also primary in sustaining professional learning communities. Time and energy must be spent on monitoring and strengthening those interactions.

Starting the Year

How do you start the year? How do you meet a new faculty in a new school? Do you set expectations for learning early and often? We have been involved with several schools where the first meeting with the faculty is one of the most important events for a principal. It is a time to set the agenda for the year. In schools where principals start the year, after introductions and housekeeping, by talking about high-performing schools and initiating a discussion about those attributes, staff members have a clearer vision of what is needed to work as a community of professional learners to increase impact on student learning. Discussing the evidence that says we are acting in alignment with our principles of professional learning communities is important in two ways: (1) it helps evaluate whether or not we are reaching our goal, and (2) it keeps the conversation focused on what our goal is for our staff. This discussion provides feedback and specific behaviors that enhance our learning.

Faculty members say that having discussions about learning at the opening of the school year and having learning conversations on an ongoing basis are good clues of school climate. Set the tone early and often.

We have a cautionary word about vision and how it is used in schools. In some schools, as well as other businesses and communities, the word *vision* has been overused. The need for vision is strong. However, keep in mind the vision is under construction during the process of dialogue in the learning communities. Stay focused on the outcomes we want for our staff, but stay open to how to get there. As we talk and learn together, the vision gets clearer. We must stay open to slight changes and new strategies and tactics that we learn along the way that could make a difference.

Using Time Opportunities

So, how much time do you spend talking about the vision, the preferred future of the school? Where do you talk about it? Are you taking every opportunity to keep it in plain sight? Is learning your vision? Would others say that learning is your vision?

The ongoing conversations you have with kids, colleagues, and community are the most important thing you can do as principal or teacher leader. Even the brief conversations that happen in the hallway on the way to solve a problem can be opportunities for anchoring and strengthening the vision for learning. A "one-legged interview" can be another way of making a point of learning, even though it is not a long conversation. A one-legged interview (sometimes called a "one-legged conference") is an informal, brief interview or discussion to learn how things are going with the implementation of a new practice or procedure. It may last only 3–5 minutes. It might take place when the principal and a group of teachers meet at the staff mailboxes for a short interlude; it might take place as the principal and several teachers walk down a hallway together; it might happen at the lunch table with a grade-level team; or it might take place in the parking lot as the principal and teachers are leaving campus. Leaders need to have their "teachable point of view" (Tichy, 1997) clearly in mind for impromptu meetings.

The Seven C's of Leadership

Leadership is important for many reasons. Following are seven elements of effective leadership—known as the Seven C's—especially related to encouraging, enhancing, and sustaining PLCs:

1. Communication

2. Collaboration

3. Coaching

4. Change

5. Conflict

6. Creativity

7. Courage

Communication

In the area of communication, are the columns you write for the student and parent newsletters focused on the vision for learning? Does the local newspaper carry articles submitted by the principal or other school leaders in which he or she advances the notion of learning? If we, as principals and other leaders, react only to issues identified in the community at large, our responses are usually reactive and after the fact. We can be proactive in getting our vision out that learning is our product, that is what we do, and that is what we are going to be accountable for to the community.

Communication opportunities arise in conferences, open houses, and parent organization meetings. How much time is spent talking to these groups about learning, which is our vision for our school? Is there a planned presentation about learning given at each event? How might you incorporate that into the existing structures?

Ultimately, communication is the message others receive, not the message we think we are sending. Being conscious how others react, how our written and oral presentations are being received, is what matters. How do you get feedback on what is being received?

Collaboration

Let's face it, it is easier to go into your classroom and teach your own way without working with anyone else. Of course, the group or system doesn't benefit from what you know, and you don't benefit from what others know.

In just about every school improvement technique and strategy that is promoted by the literature, research, and consultants, collaboration is mentioned. Everyone talks about it, and a few attempt to provide ways for collaboration to manifest itself. Collaboration is critical to the success of PLCs and most initiatives. We talk more about how to encourage collaboration in Chapter 4.

In *King Arthur's Round Table*, David Perkins (2003) describes collaboration as pooled mental work. In physical tasks, we divide up the labor, people work independently to complete their share, and the task is completed. In mental work—that is, educational issues that are ongoing—it takes mutual work toward a common goal. Perkins further indicates that some times collaboration ends up being "coblaboration." We co-talk or talk in parallel, but not much gets done. Staff collaboration about learning that positively affects student achievement is the hallmark of PLCs. Without this, we doubt whether a PLC exists. *Collegiality* is collaborating plus sharing information and feedback. Collegiality is learning and working together and toward a common purpose. Collegiality is giving and accepting feedback, which makes us better practitioners.

Another viewpoint on how organizations learn is from Etienne Wenger's book *Communities of Practice* (1998). Wenger watched how people learn their jobs in organizations. In order for employees to learn how to do their jobs, there is a need for organizational learning that is distributed throughout the organization so that everyone benefits, not just those involved in the initial learning. Wenger posits three critical steps. The first step is *mutual engagement*—the leaders must get the people in the same location so they can talk to each other.

The second step is *negotiated meaning*, which means people must be able to talk to each other without blame or shame. For example, in workshops for many years we have asked if anyone is against quality education. No one, to this point, has answered "Yes." Then, we ask people to describe quality education. As you can imagine, the diversity of thoughts, values, and beliefs vary with the size of the group. Everyone has good points. If we are not open to hearing others' points of view, we are limited by our own thoughts and perceptions.

The last step is *shared repertoire* or getting people to share their expertise with each other. This is how group wisdom gets transferred throughout the organization. This is one the most important parts of PLCs. The school must benefit from the learning of each individual and group.

Coaching

The term *coaching* is losing its original interpretation. In the 1980s, the term *coaching* was used as an alternative to *supervision* and *evaluation*. In 1994, Costa and Garmston (2002) coined the term "Cognitive Coaching." The intent was to incorporate cognition, reflective thinking, and the process of learning conversations to increase knowledge, skills, and application of learning and teaching. Clarity about what coaching is and is not is critical for those involved.

In the late 1980s, with their first edition of *Student Achievement Through Staff Development*, Joyce and Showers (1988) connected the results on student achievement and application with different training models: lecture, demonstration, modeling, practice and feedback, and coaching. Their conclusion as late as 2002, in their third edition, was that without ongoing conversations—coaching if you will—there will be little if any transfer of new knowledge and skills to the classroom or the teacher's instructional practice.

Leaders must be able to model, conduct, and sustain ongoing conversation around learning and teaching to sustain the implementation of PLCs and to increase results for student achievement. More information on specific skills is addressed in Chapters 4 and 5.

As the National Staff Development Council (NSDC) continues to advocate, staff development is professional learning and requires three things: it must be ongoing (continuous learning conversations), job embedded (meaningful to your work), and results driven (how do you know we are making progress?). Without ongoing conversations, we are limited in the scope and depth of any initiative.

Change

Any initiative involves change. Leaders are called on to lead change. There are multiple resources about leading change. Chapter 1 has already laid the foundation of leading any change initiative with its definition of a PLC. The first prerequisite for change to occur is that the staff believes change can happen. If staff members think change can occur, there is a high probability that new ways of working together can be implemented.

As stated previously, there must be a preferred future, a vision, of what we want to see. With that, staff members must see a pathway, or the steps for the vision to become a reality. From our experience, people need to see how they can get to a different future.

Changing from the way a school operates to a PLC is neither easy nor quick. We think principals and other leaders must be knowledgeable about change, how change occurs, and how to sustain a new way of doing business. In order to monitor and increase sustainability, we refer you to the Concerns-Based Adoption Model, commonly known as CBAM (Hall & Hord, 2006). CBAM includes tools to assess change and to determine the specific level of intervention for the emotional side of change as well as the behavioral side.

Change is sometimes accompanied by conflict. When new processes are encouraged, people don't feel as secure as they did with the old way of doing things. An activity we use is folding your arms in front of you. Now, take the arm that is on top and put it on the bottom, and the one on the bottom, put it on top. Does it feel uncomfortable? Probably. Change is uncomfortable, at least at the beginning. However, if you continued to fold your arms in this new way, this would feel comfortable, and the old way would start feeling uncomfortable.

Conflict

Because change is uncomfortable, sometimes this creates conflict. PLCs are hard work. This can be a stressor in life. PLCs when operating effectively create trusting environments in which smart people with good intentions can disagree honestly. If trust is not present, staff members sometimes get dug into positions, which can lead to emotional conflict.

Amason, Thompson, Hochwarter, and Harrison (1995) suggest that highly effective organizations manage conflict by accepting, discussing, and honoring differences of opinions and the individual talents of all members. Less effective organizations have conflict that tends to be emotional, based on fear and/or triangulation. How an organization manages conflict can be a major indicator of the health of the organization, whether the leadership can establish safe, honest discussions, and whether or not the organization is learning.

Principals and other leaders must *manage* conflict, not necessarily eliminate conflict. We want strong, passionate people in education. Since there is not one way to teach every child, there is not one way that is best for every student. How we honor and encourage diversity of teaching strategies, invite differences of opinions, and learn from the hard work of the individual in schools while managing conflict is discussed in subsequent chapters.

Creativity

Schools that are PLCs or are becoming PLCs offer many opportunities to address challenges creatively. Time is the foremost issue or challenge school leaders will face. Creating time for people to meet is difficult in our high-demand environments. Having a school schedule that is constant can be very stabilizing, but it can also prevent staff from working together. Principals and other leaders will have to be innovative to create space and time for meeting and collaboration.

As a new way to implement staff development, professional learning communities can be threatening to some staff members and principals. School leaders must find creative ways to introduce PLCs and be part of the PLC with staff. Administrators who model PLCs for staff signal that this is a good learning process for all levels of school personnel. An ideal situation is created when there are central office administrators who can model PLCs for building leaders.

Although our definition of professional learning community from Chapter 1 implies that only professional staff are part of the PLC, there are possibilities for parents, students, noncertified staff, advisors, and coaches to be involved in a PLC as well. The application of PLC principles suggests a variety of opportunities. To encourage creativity we ask, Could a class operate as a PLC? How about a custodial group, food service, transportation? How might staff development, school improvement plans, site-based management, and such be combined into a PLC? Sometimes it is "out of the box" thinking, sometimes it is "in the box" thinking that can provide school change solutions.

Courage

Leaders are tested continuously. If PLCs are to be implemented, it will take courage to challenge existing systems, courage to make the case for improving student outcomes, and continued courage to stay on message as to why the school is implementing a PLC. Having courage isn't easy, but it is extremely important in school change and improvement. Many initiatives come and go. PLCs have shown great promise to improve teaching and learning. However, if they are to be sustained in a school community, principals and other leaders will have to monitor progress, participate as a partner, and communicate the results.

Leaders deserve the positive staff and student outcomes that result from a PLC. Staff deserve the support and learning that can result from being part of a PLC. Students deserve the best instruction we can offer, and improved instruction is the result of collaborative staff effort as a PLC. After all, how we learn together is a great predictor of how students learn together.

The Principal's Role in Professional Development and Learning

The following scenario happens in schools more often than we would like to admit. The scene is right after winter break. You have a staff development day coming up either at the end of the month or in February or March. The question is, Whom can we bring in for that day? We have the day scheduled on the calendar as a staff development day; we have to have someone speak to our staff. What will we do? Most of us have been part of such discussions with a leadership team or a professional development committee.

An Alternative to a Staff Development Day

You don't have staff development without people development. So, how do you develop your staff members? Shirley Hord said years ago, "Staff development is not an event." This statement continues to be proven true. How many principals, with or without the professional development committee, plan staff development events? Joyce and Showers (2002) state that if you are going to host talking heads, there will be little, if any, transfer to the classroom. If there are not ongoing conversations, there will be little application of ideas or behaviors that will affect teaching and learning. We know through National Staff Development Council standards that professional learning must be ongoing, job embedded, and results driven. How does your professional learning rate on these three elements?

Leadership Implications

One of the roles for the principal is that of the change agent. Creating, implementing, and sustaining professional learning committees are not easy tasks for the change agent. To stay focused on learning, keep the vision alive in communications and actions, and align professional development to support the change takes energy and a willingness to confront tough issues. Leadership is not for the faint of heart.

To change how we do business takes committed staff and a principal who is willing to provide support to those helping implement changes. In order to implement PLCs, there have to be clear expectations of what will be required for the time given, what structures need to be in place (Chapter 3), and how the PLCs will be evaluated (Chapter 6). If you are going to change meeting times, goals for learning, procedures for learning together, and how to evaluate the learning, it will require leadership and shared vision. Staff must understand the goals for professional learning communities and the processes for implementation. These issues must be addressed upfront so everyone has clarity.

Also, keep in mind the change process. The Concerns-Based Adoption Model (Hall & Hord, 2006; Hord et al., 2004) assesses the concerns people experience as they move through the change process. First and foremost is, What is this change and how does this change affect me? When moving the school toward PLC, that is the question that kept surfacing over and over in a school where we worked. Staff wanted to know how it affected them. As principal, that question must be answered either directly or indirectly before implementation will move forward. Second, once people become comfortable with how they will be affected, they want to know what they have to do. What is the task they have to perform? And, last, how might this make a difference for the school, the kids, each other? For every change, the staff will go through these stages, and the principal must help the staff through those stages. We have not experienced any way to short-circuit this process.

Three styles of principals have been identified. In Hall and Hord's work (2006) the styles of the principal are discussed as well as how change is sustained. One style of principal is the *responder*. This principal just reacts to every issue that comes in the door. Staff, students, and parents like that; they get immediate attention. The principal is pleasant but does not focus on learning. This style does little to move a school toward collegial learning and collaboration.

The second style is *manager*. The principal reacts to issues and manages proactively. The school runs well, the schedules are accurate, the budget is in place, and the school is maintained. The school is a good place to work. However, not much change is sought nor initiated, nor are teachers encouraged to adopt new practices.

The third style is that of an *initiator*. This means the principal is consistently talking about students and programs to benefit students, initiating change, leading changes, and participating in monitoring the effects of the change. Issues get resolved, the building runs well, and the principal is focused on learning and, with the collaboration of the staff, sets the vision for the school. The principal is continually aligning practices with learning as the goal.

We would like to add a fourth principal style to this model: the role of the principal as a *collaborator.* Sometimes an initiator gets moved to another building, retires, gets sick, and in some cases, dies. We certainly don't want anything sinister to happen to educators, but such is the reality of life. We think the collaborator style adds one more dimension in which everyone is a leader, which happens by building shared leadership among the staff. This collaborative leader creates a more sustainable advantage, develops a succession plan, and can lead to long-term positive consequences for staff, students, and the community.

Leadership makes a difference. As Sparks (2005) states,

> Leaders matter. What leaders think, say, and do—and who they are when they come to work each day—profoundly affects organizational performance, the satisfaction they and those with whom they interact derive from their work, and their ability to sustain engagement with their work over the period of time necessary to oversee significant improvements. (p. vii)

Vignette

A Request

The principal can lead discussions by asking questions, making observations, or making requests. An example would be a principal's participation on a district leadership team. The principal observed that we spend two to three hours twice a month in these meetings. After three months with this district, the principal asked for time to talk. He said, "I have an observation and a request. My observation is that we must not believe learning is our most important product." A couple of people were shocked by that statement. They responded citing the mission statement, test scores, and all the problems the district was facing. The principal responded by asking, "How much time in the past three months have we talked about learning?" Heads went down because the team could remember only one hour in the past three months when learning and instruction were discussed. Then, the principal made a request: Dedicate at least one hour at each meeting to talk about learning and instruction. His request was met with a chorus of "We have so much other stuff to do" and other objections. However, after that initial observation to the whole group, there was more discussion about curriculum, instruction, and assessment. Sometimes raising the consciousness level will have positive results. Additionally, the weekly meetings of the area superintendents and staff began allocating time on the agenda in each meeting to discuss learning. The deputy superintendent made it happen, and she was honored for that action.

Rocks in the Road

Staying focused on what is important is very difficult in the daily operations of a school. Bennis (1989) writes about two laws that are applicable to schools.

Bennis's First Law of Academic Pseudodynamics. Routine work drives out nonroutine work and smothers all creative planning and fundamental change in any institution.

Keeping routine work to a minimum and focusing on learning and the cultural norms that promote learning is an awesome task. It will be the principal's biggest challenge: putting attention on things that matter most. The principal has to sort quickly and constantly to think whether his or her actions on a given subject will promote learning. If presented with a problem to solve that doesn't have major impact on learning, the principal should solve it quickly and move on. Students, staff, and parents may bring up issues they think are connected to learning. The principal must make moment-to-moment decisions about whether or not the issue is important.

As principal, you will have to become more adept at sorting out those things that make a difference from those things that are single issues. Principals could spend all of their time doing paperwork and solving all sorts of conflicts not related to learning. If those things take most of your time and attention, it will probably be at the expense of modeling and leading learning in the school. If you get accolades for solving problems, you will tend to do more of it.

How do we balance, as Stephen Covey (1989, p. 151) says, the urgent and the important? Principals have become firefighters, not educational leaders. Firefighters are on the front line dealing with crises and unfolding emergencies. We know that buses have to run, schools have to be physically and emotionally safe, and that budgets have to be monitored. Now we are advocating for time and energy designated to instructional leadership. We suggest that time is your most valuable nonrenewable resource. Your time and where you choose to spend it will signal importance to everyone in your school.

Bennis's Second Law of Academic Pseudodynamics. Make whatever grand plans you will, but you may be sure the unexpected or the trivial will disturb and disrupt them.

Because we are in an environment of such frenetic pace, like firefighters we have to make decisions very fast. The unexpected will always occur. Klein (1998) writes that when firefighters, EMTs, and operating room personnel were studied, they found that fire commanders make about 80 percent of their decisions in the first two minutes of a crisis. We believe this is similar in the principalship.

Klein suggests two strategies. The first is *pattern recognition*. The more experience a principal has, the more the principal can anticipate and proactively manage issues. The experienced principal knows what will be important or have long-term consequences. Such principals also know what to let go of, since it will be an immediate concern to someone but not a big issue in the grand scheme of things. Learning is a big issue. Learning is the major focus.

The second way to prepare people is *mental simulation*—exercises that describe real situations. Yes, you should discuss how you might approach an issue to keep the focus on what is important: student learning. Talk about how to do that during self-reflection and with others. Do you as a principal regularly discuss with your colleagues how you are keeping the focus on learning at your school? Does it appear on administrative agendas within your school or at district meetings?

Engage in Learning Activities

1. There is a French proverb that says, "Children need models more than critics." Principals must model what we want to see in schools. Gandhi's quote also comes to mind: "Be the change you want to see in the world."

Write a sentence or two for each question following. Some of the first questions a principal must answer are

- How am I modeling learning?
- How does the staff know that learning is our most important product?
- Do staff and students see me learning? Do they hear me talking about learning?
- How do you rate yourself as a learner? How would the staff and students rate you as a learner?
- How am I helping to create a professional learning community in my school? In my district?

2. Here are some questions for you to consider as you think about leading and spending your time focused on learning. Write a sentence or two to respond to each question.

- How much of my time is spent talking about and actively engaging in learning during my daily professional life?

- Are there articles about learning in every newsletter and parent information packet that goes home? To the media?
- How am I creating ongoing, job-embedded, results-driven professional learning for staff?
- How do I get feedback from students about what makes learning more effective?
- Do the district meetings I attend make sure part of the agenda includes learning discussions that would support professional learning communities?

Now discuss your statements with a trusted colleague in your school.

Now that we are on the trip, things happen. How do we work together, under what conditions will we modify our plans, and what are the nonnegotiables? To make a trip efficient and effective might be the first goal. This is especially important if we are in new territory. When we go to a new area, we want to make sure we cover as much as possible. To do that we must have some guidelines to follow so we don't waste time. We may not spend enough time on certain places because we want to cover all of the new land.

A major issue when traveling is how much time to spend doing what things. What are your roles and responsibilities when visiting places? If you travel with family or friends, it is a constant negotiation about how much time and what to include. Some want to shop; some want to sit by the beach, hike, or golf; and others want to just drive around. Time management is difficult to deal with in groups.

Another issue that comes up when traveling is different regulations in different places. If you travel abroad, you do not have the same rules as in the United States. Even going to another state can be different. There are cultural norms to be aware of, and the local customs can be confusing. It is normally easy to tell a visitor from a local. We visit the state of Hawaii every year. The locals are amused by some of our "go everywhere and do everything" attitude.

3

Culture and Context, Structures and Schedules, Policies and Procedures

Our principal just shared with the school improvement team that the state board of education is strongly urging the legislature to require all schools to create a professional community of learners in each school in the state! That would help us to maintain our professional community in our school.

Assistant principal in a high school

Well there's no way for this staff to develop a community of learning professionals—they don't even have time scheduled in the day for planning their lessons.

Secretary at an elementary school

I would be glad to have my children's school day extended most days and shortened one day a week so teachers could stay current with the latest research on how to teach effectively. I believe it would prepare them to help my challenged twin to be a better reader.

Parent of two middle school students

I n Chapter 1, we reported outcomes for staff and students in schools where the professionals on the staff work as professional learning communities (PLCs). While those faculty results and related student outcomes are exciting, creating the PLC requires a great deal of energy, commitment, and elbow grease. In Chapter 2, we addressed the imperative of the principal, for it is this leader, as noted in Chapter 1, who is the gatekeeper to change. As the gatekeeper, the principal is the key to whether and if a school develops a community of learning professionals who continually review and revise the school's curriculum and instructional strategies for student benefits. The principal and other school leaders nurture a context wherein continuous learning is the *modus operandi* for staff and students and provides a broad range of structures and resources to support the staff in learning their new practices.

If the school operates in a context of assessment and continuous improvement, such an environment supports the initiation and development of a professional learning community. But basic structures and schedules may need rearranging so that grade-level teams and subject matter departments can come together to learn and participate in collegial learning. This is tricky, but the real challenge is finding the time so that *all* the professionals in the school work together to identify goals that reflect student needs, and then learn new content and strategies to realize those goals.

Not only is time an issue in most schools, but in some schools space is lacking. This also contributes to difficulties in staff meeting together. And, of course, not all the staff recognize the value of spending time with colleagues to become more effective and efficient. Thus, building collaborative relationships among the staff can be a significant challenge. Along with time and space, how teachers are organized in the school, structures within the meetings—such as an agenda, recording the minutes, and so on—contribute additionally to the complexity of initiating and maintaining a professional learning community.

In this chapter we are thinking again about the graphic that depicts our theory of how professional learning relates to student learning (refer again to Figure 1.3). Particularly, we focus on Box 4 of that figure and discuss the importance of developing a PLC culture and providing necessary structures, policies, and procedures to support and sustain the PLC.

Someone must be responsible for these requirements and for the resources that are needed. That someone initially is the principal, but these responsibilities should be shared with the community as it develops. Failure to give attention to the structures, resources, and relationships will doom the community to failure. This chapter addresses the "nuts and bolts" already mentioned and focuses on how individuals at the campus level provide support for the PLC. In short, we address the context in which the PLC will be born and grow. In so doing, we discuss the structural and the relational requirements and the supports that the PLC needs to function well:

How do context, climate, and culture impact the PLC setting?

What factors of the infrastructure at the school influence the PLC?

How do policies and normative practices boost or deenergize the PLC?

What resources—material and human—are required?

In this chapter, the focus is on the principal and other leaders who engineer and provide the contextual requirements for effectively functioning PLCs. We begin with a very brief historical review of the literature to inform us about experts' perspectives on culture and context, in order to gain meaning and understanding of these vital concepts and their application to PLC.

The Culture in the Context

Culture is embedded in a school and/or district's context, maintained Boyd (1992), from a review of the corporate and school literature. The *culture* comprises the people or human factors; the *context* is comprised of the ecological factors or situational variables (physical or structural factors) in the setting. But, what really is culture? Many writers are making much of this dimension of the organization, especially in schools (Barth, 2006; Fullan, 2001; Hargreaves, 2003).

In early work on culture, Harris (1968) noted that "the culture concept comes down to behavior patterns associated with particular groups of people . . . or to a people's 'way of life'" (p. 16). Spradley (1979) proposed that "culture . . . refers to the acquired knowledge that people use to interpret experience and generate social behavior" (p. 5). Schein (1992) maintained:

The culture of a group can be defined as a pattern of shared basic assumptions that the group learned . . . that has worked well enough to be considered valid and, therefore, to be taught to new members as the correct way to perceive, think, and feel in relation to [the organization's] problems. (p. 12)

Further, culture is the individually and socially constructed values, norms, and beliefs about an organization and how it should behave. The culture and the situational variables interact to make up the context. While culture is commonly thought of as "the way things are done around here," climate is the way people feel about the way things are done. *Climate* is the individuals' perceptions of the work setting and derives from the context and its embedded culture. First, a brief look at culture.

The PLC Culture

From the five characteristics of a professional learning community described in Chapter 1, one can easily visualize some aspects of the culture that develops when staff work as a PLC. There are shared values among the staff members that provide the parameters for a vision for change that will benefit students. Shared and supportive leadership that nurtures the development of leadership across the staff (think here, distributed or inclusive leadership) results in shared power, authority, and decision making. This is not a top-down, mandated-decisions culture, but a highly cooperative and collaborative setting in which the community (defined by shared purpose) studies problems and decides democratically how to solve them.

Relationships in the community are based on mutual regard, respect, and caring. Attitudes are such that there is shared concern about all members of the professional community and the additional staff and students at the campus. The matter of relationships constitutes a significant variable of the culture, which is centered on the people and the human factors in the community.

These relationships are more positive and thus more powerful when they are characterized by reflection, porosity, and transparency. Think

Mirrors for reflection

Membranes for porosity

Windows for transparency

That is, when the staff members in the school reflect individually and collectively about their work and its benefits for students, their work is more thoughtfully directed to desired student outcomes. When they interact with each other in an open and porous way, ideas can move more readily from one individual or grade level or department to others. When the spoken expressions and behaviors of the professionals are transparent and authentic, then trust can develop. Research has shown clearly that trust is a basic requirement for people in the school to work productively and pleasantly together (Bryk & Schneider, 2002). Reflection, porosity, and transparency contribute to the increase of the organization's flexibility and resilience.

Because the culture and its need for attention to relationships is such a strong tenet of the PLC and requires much of the principal's attention, it is a thread woven throughout the following chapters. We introduce it here to note the fact that the culture is part of the context and the setting in which the PLC operates. In the PLC, we are moving from a culture of isolation to a culture of adult learning and collegiality.

Focus on the Vision of Change

One of the enduring problems in many schools is the lack of a consistent focus or direction for improvement. These schools are burdened by too big a plateful of programs and processes that teachers never learn to use productively, so they never reach implementation. School improvement consultant Larry Lezotte suggested "prioritized abandonment" (personal communication, no date) wherein a school identifies its major goal and uses the goal as a critical assessment for whether or not each of the school's multiple programs should be left on the plate.

In schools where there is a culture of continuous improvement and where staff are examining their work, setting goals for student learning, and deciding what they need to learn in order for students to become more successful learners, the goal or focus is kept squarely in front of everyone. Parents and students know what this focus is and can report to school visitors; faculty members are learning how to address the goal with specific content knowledge and instructional strategies. As mentioned in Chapter 1, one of the principal's major activities is to keep this focus alive and to engage others in doing likewise. This means the principal and other leaders "stay on message" frequently and consistently. You will hear this again in Chapter 4. Maintaining focus keeps everyone moving in the same direction, albeit with possible variations in the movement. While articulating clear goals and keeping a focus on the goals is of prime importance, allowing for some flexibility in how to reach the goals is also important. Creative people are not happy to be bound to "one way" to accomplish the objective or goal; they should have the option of finding their way to succeed with the goal.

Expectations

When there is a clear focus and a definite plan to reach quality implementation of the new work that the staff will adopt together, expectations are apparent to all. From these expectations the staff takes its clues about new content and instructional practices they need to learn. When a faculty undertakes new practices unsuccessfully, they often lack understanding of what the new practice will look like when it has been implemented well. Clarity of the focus for change and clear descriptions of what administrators, teachers, students, and others involved will be doing allows all to be informed about what is expected for all individuals with the new work that has been agreed upon. Having this shared vision that spells out the actions that will be taken decreases frustrations, annoyances, and disappointments. Being precise about expectations is a boon to be shared by all in the community. However, there will always be good reasons for changing the road map or the destination, so flexibility, as noted already, should be part of the journey.

Decision Making and Conflict Resolution

Most school staff members have not had the privilege of shared decision making and must learn how to exercise this important responsibility. One would not turn a first grade classroom loose to use learning centers without first providing instruction and practice about the appropriate way to "do" centers. Oftentimes it is assumed that faculty know how to make decisions. Don't you just vote? Well, of course you could, but in using this decision-making process, some win and others lose. There are better ways to make decisions that preserve positive relationships among the staff.

In professional learning communities, members are expected to be open and to share opinions. In the community, "teachers tolerate (even encourage) debate, discussion and disagreement" (Wignall, 1992). When such openness occurs, there is bound to be an occasional conflict. At this point, the community uses the skill that it has developed for managing and resolving conflict. The wise leader does not wait for conflict to erupt before addressing processes for resolving conflict within the community. Perhaps there are teachers who have developed these skills, and they can instruct their colleagues on the processes.

Staff Development Opportunities and Restrictions

Collective learning is one of the five attributes of the professional learning community, and, as such, focuses squarely on the priority purpose of the PLC. The PLC is uniquely situated to provide quality professional development to the community's members. Quality professional development occurs in many venues: two teachers working on an instructional plan for one or many students; grade-level teams working together to create high intellectual learning tasks for students; the whole staff reflecting on their work with students, identifying areas for improvement, and determining what they, the staff, need to learn in order for their students to become more successful learners. This professional learning is the heart and soul of the PLC. Thus, staff learning with each other is encouraged in many ways, in many places, and at many times. So that all of the "ships are sailing in the same direction," it is important for the entire school professional community to come together regularly and frequently to learn and to ensure this happens.

The "beliefs we hold and the values we share, the way we do things around here" are reflected in the culture, and impact all the individuals who are part of the particular community. But the context also influences how people work in community—or in isolation. The culture and the context are interactive. We turn next to context variables and how they affect PLC.

Aspects of the Campus Infrastructure: The Context

The relationships in many of the schools that we know are characterized by staff members as a "we/they" situation where the school administrators exist in one environment and the teaching staff in another. There is lack of open communication, schedules are unpredictable, and space for community work is unstable. These are just a few of the factors that contribute to the success or failure of a PLC, but they are critical to the PLC's effectiveness.

Information Flow

Communication structures are vital to a well-functioning PLC. So that everyone can be involved meaningfully in decision making about curriculum, instruction, and other teaching and learning activities, a wide range of information—excluding that which is confidential and would be harmful to students or staff—should be shared. Almost uniformly in poor performing schools, there is the complaint about not knowing what is expected of educators' performance or what educators can expect of the system. Well-developed communication structures support the professional learning community so that everyone is informed about schedules, budgets, upcoming issues and events, and so on. Schools use a variety of structures to promote information sharing and communication.

Meetings

The old familiar faculty meeting was conducted mainly to be an information-sharing event. Time was used indiscriminately to announce holidays, the theme for the senior prom, and dates for the Bloodmobile's appearance on a corner of the campus. Seldom was the weekly faculty meeting used for more substantive purposes. Most of the information conveyed could have been done by e-mail or the "Notes From the Principal About the Week's Events." It should be obvious that we prefer such material to be sent by wireless or paper, leaving the hard-to-schedule meetings for more thought-requiring work and discussions about learning. Nonetheless, information is important to people, and a system for sharing it must be devised.

E-mail or the Circular Note

Most schools now are wired and professional staff members have access to a computer by which they can receive daily or hourly communication from the front office. On the other hand, in those schools that are not wired, a note can be carried around to the staff. This is one way to make information available, but when it arrives unannounced, it easily intrudes negatively on the instructional process in classrooms. Further, no time is allowed for absorbing the information. We believe this structure is not a good one. An alternative scheme is the placement of notes in faculty mailboxes. In this case, faculty are free to take their copy, review it, and make appropriate notes to themselves about it.

Using e-mail for the purpose of transferring information is a time-saving and paper-saving way to share information. It also provides the means by which each individual can respond immediately and quickly; this communication structure also offers the possibility for interaction across the community and sharing of responses. Of course, this means that each classroom or small group of classrooms will require the equipment and the necessary training for the staff to use it. Some teachers will frequently wish to have a hard copy in their hands, and this can be accommodated if a printer is made available as part of the suite of equipment.

Newsletter

A more formalized communication scheme for sharing information and for various other purposes, such as invitations, soliciting responses to surveys, or announcing upcoming state achievement tests, is the school newsletter. This document may be disseminated weekly, monthly, semimonthly, or whatever calendar is feasible and desirable. Such newsletters frequently contain an article from each of the school's grade levels or academic departments. It may contain students' work such as poems, short stories, or essays. These bulletins can be distributed to all teachers, students, and families. The newsletter is an effort to inform everyone. To ensure that families actually receive it, mailing it would probably be important, as such items tend to disappear from students' backpacks while en route home. These newsletters may be placed in staff mailboxes so that everyone is informed and has hard copy to save and/or mark for specific attention.

The flow of information is vital to the community's success. This flow should be not only vertical—from and to the front office—but also horizontal, for instance, across grade level and academic department teachers. Communication structures that promote reflection, transparency, and porosity provide valuable means by which all members of the community are informed. The structures mentioned here contribute to that knowledge base that everyone should have. The principals have the responsibility to initiate these structures. Members of the community share in these tasks as they develop their work together.

Time and Space

A major challenge that the community must solve is time to meet for learning and to do their collaborative work. Many schools note that they can't develop into communities of professional learners because they don't have the time needed. A few schools seem not to be able to allocate space for community meetings and collegial work. This is another structural issue.

Time

This four-letter word is a barrier to PLCs, and it is truly a problem that is difficult to solve. The profession and the public seem to expect school staffs to "fly the plane and redesign its features" simultaneously. Thus, providing time for staff to come together, to study and deliberate, make thoughtful decisions, and plan to implement the decisions is sometimes a nightmare. Some schools beseech their districts to allow or provide time so that it is regularly scheduled for community work across the district for all schools. This can be done by extending 4 days of the weekly instructional time and identifying an early release day for students, while faculty remain in the school for professional learning and collaborative work. This would seem to be the best way to access the time, but it does require gaining parents' understanding and union approval, dealing with bus schedules and the instructional schedule. Some schools have an early period of the day in which parents substitute in classes and the faculty meets together in community. This approach would be dependent on state and/or district policies that allow parents to participate in this way. Another example is the use of staff development budgets to hire substitutes to cover classes. Some school administrators have found money to support an early evening meal to "sweeten" an after-school meeting of the community. Breaking bread together helps the participants feel valued and energizes them after a long day. For more ideas, see Table 3.1. It suggests ways to add time that were considered by schools working to become PLCs during a project supported by the Southwest Educational Development Laboratory called "Creating Communities of Continuous Inquiry and Improvement." We also suggest that you take a look at the spring 1999 and spring 2007 issues of the *Journal of Staff Development*, published by the National Staff Development Council. These issues are dedicated to the challenges of finding or creating time and cover slightly different topics.

Providing the time for the *entire* staff to meet as a *whole school PLC* is essential. Grade-level or academic subject professional learning teams are worthwhile structures. However, if the whole school community does not work together, the goals, purposes, and activities of the individual teams may be moving willy-nilly in various and opposite directions, as in Scenario A in Figure 3.1. The larger school PLC allows for the smaller team units to do specific work (of importance to the grade level or academic subject area), but also maintain movement toward common schoolwide goals and mission, as in Scenario B.

Space

At one school that we know, where a fully developed learning community of professionals worked, the school's student population was expanding. The area where the professionals had their lunch together and met for their collegial learning meetings was being considered for use as a classroom. The educators thought long and hard

Figure 3.1   Aligning Subgroup Activities With Whole School Goals

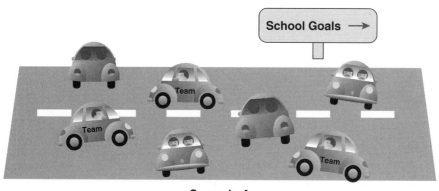

Scenario A

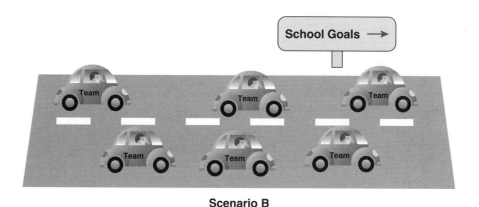

Scenario B

about this possibility and its consequences. They finally concluded that the best interests of their students resided in their knowledge and skills, and that increasing their effectiveness would be diminished if they lost this space for this purpose.

Another school that was extended over 40 acres in 40 buildings found it difficult to bring educators together for learning together and collaborative work. Proximity was the problem. The community solved this by furnishing all members a blueprint of the campus with the charge to develop a landscape that would put educators in closer communication and contact with each other. Giving the community the problem to solve was the obviously appropriate method, and, incidentally, is a good way to initiate the launch of a PLC. Other PLCs have met in the band room, in the cafeteria after hours, and on the auditorium stage. One principal initiated a creative and

Table 3.1   Ways to Increase Time

Co-Developer Meeting Creating Communities of Continuous Inquiry and Improvement Project Southwest Educational Development Laboratory March 1999

- Longer school day four days per week with time "saved" used another day for professionals to meet, study, plan.
- Extend each day of the week by 10 minutes for an early or late start or to provide a periodic release day.
- Extend the school day by ½ hour on Monday, Tuesday, Thursday, Friday; on Wednesday (midweek) PLC staff are involved in professional development and dialogue, and so on from 8 to 10:30. Students arrive at 10:30 for modified day: thematic work, community activities, field trips, community assistance exchanges.
- Bank time by choosing one hour per week before or after school in study groups—compensated by districtwide professional development days.
- Consider the possibility of gaining time from scheduled lunch periods.
- Add minutes to beginning and end of four days—give ½ day off to students on fifth day.
- Bank time by adding minutes per day—yields ½ day for professional development per semester.
- Cut down on passing time to build time available for PLC to meet one afternoon per week or month.
- "School day" becomes "school week" with beginning and ending hours of each day flexible for schools.
- Extend to eight-hour workday for teachers, principals, and all others supporting teaching and learning.
- Extend school year to gain days.
- Extend the school year and "plant" planning days and professional development throughout the year.
- Use state staff development days to create time throughout the year.
- Come an hour early or stay an hour late—this is once a week over time—when district gives a workday you don't have to come. Documentation is necessary.
- PLC meets before school.
- PLC meets on a Saturday or after school, and this can replace a professional day.
- Pay for Saturday PLC members' time.
- Meet beyond the "contract" day by being able to leave early on another day.
- Provide waivers for instructional contact hours.

- Handle administrative matters in writing to free up meeting time for staff learning.
- Reconsider the use of scheduled faculty meetings.
- Teachers from one grade level invite students in for "buddy work" with older kids, teachers from lower grade meet together; trade off the next week (or day).
- Students of teams of teachers do volunteer community work—frees that team of teachers for study and work together.
- Stipends from grants for release, or extra compensation.

meaningful response to the space problem by rotating the meetings of the community around the teachers' classrooms. This not only provided the space but gave the participants access to other teachers' rooms, where they modestly learned what and how the resident teacher was teaching and gained useful instructional strategies for their own use.

Another structural issue focuses on how classrooms are arranged and how the educators within the school are organized. In many schools of current design, classrooms are arranged in "pods" to facilitate interaction among the teachers housed in the pod, typically by grade levels, by departments, or as interdisciplinary teams. This means that teachers' work and interaction areas are frequently in the center of the pod, with classrooms arranged around this core. This design makes it easy to provide community use of technology, to create libraries for the particular department's use, and other professional possibilities. In addition, this area could contain a sofa, easy chair, and magazine table to add warmth and comfort to the pod's appeal and efficiency. Such arrangements, of course, do not happen by magic, but by the imaginative and energetic work of significant people on the campus. The principal? You bet. But teachers also can contribute to creatively addressing the issue of space.

In one school where PLC was being introduced, the administrators brought the special education classrooms into the building from the "portables" where they had been housed. This move communicated the value that was placed on all educators in the school and gave the special ed teachers better access to the regular ed teachers. Where was space found for the special ed classes that had formerly been outside the main building? The administrators moved their offices into the main hallway near the entrance to the school, so that they would be accessible to all and available to staff and visitors. But the major reason was to make space for the special ed classes and to make the administrators' tasks and roles more visible and transparent to all. For confidential appointments, there was a small conference room.

Policies and Normative Practice

One of the challenges or barriers to creating and maintaining a PLC is state and district regulations and union policies that regulate or limit the learning time. When the amount of time and the place for professional learning is dictated, this certainly decreases the creativity of schools as they seek to come together to learn. The learning together and planning for implementing the learning contributes powerfully to faculty morale and the confidence about their teaching, and their feelings of efficacy that they can influence students' learning.

Federal and State Mandates

The No Child Left Behind legislation has compelled educators to examine what they do, how they do it, and the effects it has on students. It has called attention to instructional assessment, to the provision of high-quality professional development, and to other issues. While such mandates are rarely embraced positively, they nonetheless gain people's attention. One of our European principals in a secondary school reported that he would blame those at the "governing level of the system" for mandating actions for the school, while he used this mandate to initiate action within the school. Mandates are not typically the most pleasant or appealing way to gain the attention of school educators, but it can work. The clue is to use the external policy handed down from above. Work with local educators, being sensitive to their concerns (Hall & Hord, 2006), and engage the staff as a community of learners in order to gain the expertise demanded of the new policies and practices. This is discussed further in Chapter 4.

State student achievement tests are the bane of many schools' existence. Peculiar, since most of these tests have been in existence for many years, assessing the acquisition of basic knowledge and skills that we want all students to possess. Many educators have only in recent years been held accountable for student results. This new expectation has been difficult for many educators and schools to understand and accept, but the state achievement tests have certainly put bite into the educational process at many schools. This process can be more comfortably and successfully conducted when administrators and teachers have the support and assistance of their colleagues. Thus, referring to the state tests can be a fruitful way to gain attention and to persuade faculty to come together to solve their testing challenges.

In addition, there are some state statutes that are recommending the establishment of PLCs in schools. This legislation certainly gives credence and power to those seeking to initiate and develop communities of professional learners in schools.

Union Regulations

How union contracts are negotiated and enforced can support the creation and development of professional learning communities or hinder the process. Unions have become increasingly aware of the importance of professional development and the learning of administrators and teachers and have put their interest and weight behind this issue. But any widespread advocacy for the establishment of PLCs in schools has yet to come from unions. Nonetheless, some local union representatives may be counted on to support this issue, or at least not interfere with it. The wise principal will solicit the local union representative's interest and support as the PLC is initiated.

Resources Required

The creation of any new entity, whether it is a physical structure, a relational arrangement, new curriculum content, or an instructional strategy, will almost certainly require resources of various kinds for its implementation, support, and maintenance. Time and space are resources, and they have already been noted. What is discussed now are the particular material and human resources needed for the development and sustainability of the professional learning community.

Material Resources

A powerful way to initiate a PLC is to supply staff with student achievement data and other archival data (for example, reports related to dropouts, absenteeism, and disciplinary incidents) for their study and review. If the test company, state, or district has not supplied data in a format for school educators' understanding and meaning making, the school may need to step up to the plate to gain access to the data in forms that are readily understandable. This may mean reformatting or reorganizing the data.

So that the community's meetings are productive and efficient, particular meeting structures should become routine. The agenda for each meeting should be published and available to all prior to the meeting, with invitations to staff to contribute to or take responsibility for specific items. Minutes of the meetings that include decisions made and/or items tabled for further discussion need to be considered. Timekeepers and reporters may require forms or directions for their tasks. In essence, structures and formats for conducting and reporting about the meeting should be in place. Two excellent resources for such protocols are Murphy and Lick (2005) and Jolly (2005).

Because the staff are becoming a community of learners, professional materials must be available. These include books that address the topics selected by the community for its learning in order to improve their instructional practice with students. Subscriptions to journals that address practices and processes for improving learning outcomes for students are recommended, since they provide insight into the new behaviors that educators will need. Several that immediately come to mind are *Educational Leadership*, produced by the Association for Supervision and Curriculum Development; the *Journal of Staff Development*, created and disseminated by the National Staff Development Council; and *Phi Delta Kappan*, often referenced by the single word, *Kappan*.

Videotapes, CDs, and DVDs from many publishers and producers visually portray teaching and organizational practices for educators, helping them to learn more explicitly about a topic of their choice. Computer programs of various types are available for study and professional learning, and Web sites that report research results can be visited. The accumulation and distribution of these materials suggests the creation of a professional library and structures for the checking out and returning of the materials. Papers presented at conferences can also be sorted and filed for access in the library for perusal and review by the community members.

In addition to paper or technological texts, there may be a need for equipment on which to use the videos, CDs, and so on. This equipment could be part of the school's inventory and available for checkout and use. If furniture for the community's meeting space is needed, this should be considered. Some schools keep a small stock of paper cups, napkins, coffee pot, sugar, and other condiments for coffee and tea. A really "flush" school may keep sodas and other beverages and snacks for the community meetings.

Human Resources

One of the goals of the professional learning community is the democratic participation of all members; thus, tasks and responsibilities should be shared. Before these become routine, the principal is the person who will be primarily responsible for seeking volunteers and delegating tasks and follow-up to see that the tasks are accomplished. An especially important role for the participants is to share in planning and guiding the learning on which the community is focusing. Often the expertise needed for enhancing the staff's instructional effectiveness resides in the school. When this expertise is internal, such expertise may be shared with the staff. If, however, the school roster does not include educators who can guide others in their learning of specific topics, then external people will be needed. These may come from central office, or another school in the district, or from persons in a nearby district. A consultant from an external assistance agency can frequently be accessed. The point is that human resources of various types may well be required. Consideration should be given to this need. Table 3.2 lists a few ideas for obtaining the human resources you need. These are ideas that schools participating in the Creating Communities of Continuous Inquiry and Improvement project developed.

Table 3.2   Ideas for Adding Human Resources

Co-Developer Meeting Creating Communities of Continuous Inquiry and Improvement Project, Southwest Educational Development Laboratory, March 1999

- Hire or reallocate staff so that there are substitutes available for staff study, work, and planning during the day.
- Use clinical or intern and resident students from university to cover classes.
- Use parent/community volunteers to allow staff to study or receive training.
- Implement "Activity Day" when students are engaged in multiple enrichment activities led by volunteer "experts" while staff meets.
- Multiage student grouping with students working on projects with trained substitutes or monitors.
- Hire one or more "permanent" subs.
- Use retirees to cover classes.
- Use trained parent, family, or community volunteers.
- Nonteaching positions cover classes.

(Continued)

(Continued)

- Cadre of substitute teachers trained to cover classes.
- Substitutes in schools for selected groups of teachers—example, grade level across district and subject level.
- Pay substitutes to teach.
- Partner teaching—where two people share one position and can sub for each other.
- Required time in each school for collaboration—subs float around the district.
- School on Wheels—a group of 25 subs and 1–2 administrators trained to move into schools and take over at any and all grade levels. They have a plan, generic to the needs of the students. Twenty-five subs usually cover an elementary, but more are usually needed for middle and high schools. One team at a time to release groups works best.
- Group all students in a grade level together for a common activity; use aide with parent volunteers to work with students; teachers for that grade level meet together.
- Recruit volunteers to manage large group activities with one certified staff to free up other teachers for time to meet and study.
- Teachers covering for other teachers.

And, what to do if the current school and district budgets don't stretch sufficiently to fill these needs? Partnerships with business or community agencies may be a good answer. Lacking ready access to such arrangements, state departments and other entities frequently issue calls for proposals that will award funds for particular projects to the successful applicants. Community members should check Web sites for possibilities. In the wise school, some members should be given the responsibility of learning to write clear and succinct proposals for grants.

Does this quick review of structures and schedules, policies and procedures, and culture and context sound daunting? There are no expectations that they be done all at once, or by a single person. That is the beauty of the PLC—the shared learning and the shared acquisition of "the stuff" required for the operation of the PLC. But how do altering the school's procedures, reallocating its resources, and working to change its culture affect the school leadership?

Leadership Implications

It is clear that the school principal will need strong talents for dealing with budgetary matters and possible fiscal restraints. Persuading the central office, superintendent, and school board to award more funds to particular projects should be pursued. Stay tuned to possible grant monies through constant surveillance of the Internet to ascertain what is available and possible. How is the principal to be in charge of all things simultaneously? Being the "jack of all trades and master of none" harbors the potential danger of doing nothing very well.

Sharing Tasks

We have seen the accommodation of many of the structural and environmental issues being shared by members of the professional community. In a southwestern state, on a cold December morning, we entered the school where we were to visit with the principal and teachers to learn about their PLC. Snow had begun to fall. Uh-oh, would we be able to accomplish our mission? Presently, a young teacher who was chairperson of the Indigenous Weather Committee approached us and reported that it appeared that the weather would be clearing shortly and that we would be able to meet the outlined schedule. The principal was nowhere to be seen. The Weather Chairperson explained that she and her four committee members had the responsibility of staying in tune with the downtown weather forecaster, and with the district's Director of Attendance to glean clues about what to do when bad weather struck. The Weather Committee was one of the school's design teams. The committee members had a job description and understood their responsibilities. These teachers shared in the management of the school.

Our first appointment that morning was with the Staff Development Design Team. This group of six teachers had carefully noted the school's improvement goals for the year, had queried each teacher to identify their needs and preferences, had reviewed the teachers' portfolios of their work, and had been given the staff development budget for the year by the principal. This committee conducted its business in a highly professional and businesslike manner. In less than an hour the committee had made proposals for what the whole faculty would engage in and approved several requests made by individual teachers for attendance at special conferences for the purpose of specific learning. The principal appeared three minutes before the meeting concluded to hear the committee's recommendations and to approve. It had been an amazing performance by a small group of very young teachers who were obviously knowledgeable about how to do their work. They were savvy and caring about their colleagues.

This principal had multiple strategies for sharing the management of material and human resources, the budget, policies emanating from the state house and district, and what the parents were concerned about. The principal consequently found time and possibilities for her own professional learning and for using that to lead the teachers in gaining new knowledge and skills.

Establishing Routines

The principal in a school in another state had persuaded one of the school community businesses to contribute simple meals at the end of a day of teaching followed by professional learning community meetings where staff were discussing needs of students and how to meet them. These teachers were so accustomed to the structures and routines established by the principal that when they entered the meeting room and saw food and chart stands by the several tables, they arranged themselves at the tables making certain that the groups had diversity of gender, ethnicity, and grade level. This principal, like the one in the southwest, had developed the structures so they became routine and time efficient, exactly what they had envisioned in their strategies to develop a PLC.

There are many ways that principals can "cover the bases" of what is needed structurally and resource-wise, with attention to policies and regulations. They do this by creative thinking, using all possibilities at their disposal, and engaging the staff in the operation. This spreads the tasks, but it also gives the faculty a feeling of participation, contribution, commitment, and ownership. It contributes to the staff's emerging management skills, supports the development of leadership opportunities for the staff, and influences the culture of the school as well.

Vignette

Garage Sale Junkies and Other Unusual Ideas

In a small K–12 rural school in a community with a population of 450 people, the staff worked diligently to learn new instructional techniques and to provide up-to-date materials and resources for their students. A new mathematics curriculum had been promoted by the state department of education and was adopted by the school. The challenging issue was the array of materials required for using the curriculum. As the teachers studied the curriculum and practiced teaching it to each other, they identified a long list of items needed, most of which were common items available in hardware stores—if you lived near one—but exceeded their budget in any case.

Reading the Saturday morning weekly newspaper, the principal noted a large garage sale advertised in the paper. The ad declared that all items were "gently" used and half or a fraction of the price of new ones. Being a connoisseur of garage sales and an aficionado of flea market opportunities, the principal jumped into his car and made fast tracks to the sale with the teachers' list of what they needed.

He perused long tables, bumping into multiple shoppers with their baskets piled high. His progress was slowed a bit by several conversations initiated by some of his school's parents, who had taken this opportunity for Saturday morning shopping. He was pleased and a bit relieved to note that none of the school board members were involved in this early morning activity.

There is no way to use a purchase order that requires quite a bit of time to make its way along the request, approval, or rejection process at a garage sale. So, using his own credit card, which probably abrogated the district policy, he happily returned home with bundles of materials and equipment that would serve the new mathematics instruction very well. He had served his teachers productively, knowing that they would be pleased at the materials and resources that he had acquired.

Moral of this story: There is more than one way to skin a cat.

Rocks in the Road

As noted previously, *time* is the barrier. It is a barrier when it is not readily available, and it is a booster when it is present. It does not appear too difficult to schedule time for grade-level and subject matter departments to meet to do collaborative work. And, such work is very important; it allows those who are closest to particular students to examine data, hear each others' observations, and make plans for how best to serve students. Many schools and districts regularly schedule team planning time daily in the teachers' work day. What is difficult is arranging time and schedules for the entire faculty (administrators and teachers) to come together to do whole school work: examining schoolwide data and coming to consensus about what the school as a whole should seek for its goals and how they will reach them. Time is not just a rock in the road to working as a professional learning community, it is a boulder!

Some administrators, predicting a negative response to a request, weigh the risks and benefits for students, move ahead, and then seek forgiveness. This may not be the best strategy in many schooling situations, but a certain amount of risk taking seems useful in working to supply the structures and schedules needed for new undertakings such as a professional learning community. Undoubtedly there will be times when existing policies and procedures will prove to be barriers and a way around them may be the only recourse. The lesson here is to be creative and inventive when things get in the way, but don't challenge the laws of the land (jail is not a nice place to be) nor the safety of oneself, faculty, students, and others.

Running amuck of the local educators' union is not a good idea; thus an acceptable idea is to develop a strong relationship with the union representative early on. Many union representatives have been very creative themselves in helping to solve regulatory issues and policies that barricade learning opportunities for staff and students. Visiting his or her office and introducing oneself also to the local legislative representative can be rewarding down the road. Cultivate good relationships with these representatives and help them to understand the problems of the school staff and how to solve them; become an advocate.

We are still learning about how to create the PLC; not much well-designed, rigorously conducted research has been done that yielded meticulously analyzed data and well-crafted reports discussing how to create PLCs. Much of what we know has been gained from the experiences and war stories of those who have tried to create this way of working in a school. This is not a bad source, but it limits our clear understanding about what actions were taken, by whom, under what conditions, with what kind of faculty, and the demographic descriptions of the students. Because these communities of professional learners are not created in the short term, conducting studies of PLCs requires substantial resources. Principals who are working on their advanced degrees could be great candidates for conducting these studies.

Engage in Learning Activities

Form a small committee with two or three principal colleagues to serve as a learning community and do the following activities:

1. Review the education bills passed by the state legislature in the past two years and note any that relate to the possible creation or

maintenance of a PLC. What policies or regulations are provided in the bills? Also note any support or resources that the bill would contribute to schools or districts that make the effort to create PLC.

2. Consult with two professional librarians and solicit recommendations from them about quality professional journals for teachers of the various subject matter courses (literacy, mathematics, science, social studies, others), and for journals that share ideas and processes for improving schools. Then request review copies and ask teachers for their opinions about the value of the journals (give the teachers a set of qualities by which to critique them). Determine if they should be purchased for the school's professional library.

3. Identify five schools that are organized as PLCs. Interview the principal and one teacher and ask them to describe what the PLC looks like in their school and how they found *time* for the PLC.

Ok, so we have read all the travel books; we are now on our adventure, and enjoying the new land. We are in a new environment, and we find out that all that reading, all the preparing, and all of the knowledge did not totally prepare us for what we find. We still want to have a good time. We have to adapt to new surroundings. What do our leaders of this trip do to make it more enjoyable?

In traveling we have found that we must stay open to learning new things in real time. We can and should prepare but always know that things will happen we didn't prepare for. We have to use what we know to make the best decisions possible when we are in new territory.

We also have to make sure we prioritize. When we try to do everything, we might not take the time to enjoy a site or an event due to rushing around. Keeping focused on the most important sites makes the trip worthwhile. We get to explain to others about our trip when we return home.

4

Creating Conditions to Get Started

Coming together is a beginning; keeping together is progress; working together is success.

Henry Ford Sr.

If we don't change, we don't grow. If we don't grow, we are not really living. Growth demands a temporary surrender of security.

Gail Sheehy

Nothing fails so much as overwhelming success.

Peter Drucker

So, professional learning communities (PLCs) are a good idea, and you want the learning that can result from collegial interaction and feedback. Now, what do you do? When a space capsule goes into space, engineers know that 90 percent of the fuel is used at lift-off. The same is true for initiating a new process or norm for professional learning communities. Overcoming status quo to initiate new ways of interacting requires lots of energy in the beginning phases. Perhaps by now you have decided PLCs are a good idea, that they could lead to making the staff more thoughtful and increase the learning among the adults. But how do you get this process started?

Edmonds (1979) wrote:

> We can, whenever and wherever we choose, successfully teach all children whose schooling is of interest to us. We already know more than we need to do that. Whether or not we do it must finally depend on how we feel about the fact that we haven't so far. (p. 23)

One of the most important preconditions for any implementation is the belief that change can happen. Once the principal and other leaders believe change is possible, that belief increases the likelihood that PLCs can be implemented and be sustained.

If we are choosing to begin learning together in a systematic way, using data to inform our practice, and are committed to reflective conversations, we will do things differently. O'Hanlon (1999) has written a book called *Do One Thing Different*. O'Hanlon's premise is that we are better served if we do one thing rather than trying to change everything at once. That may be sage advice when dealing with school change. One thing leads to another and another and so on. As Chief Seattle noted long ago, "Everything is connected."

Beckhard (1987), from the business literature, writes about change. In general, his model is that change happens when there is dissatisfaction with the current state, a compelling vision of what we could be, and a clear path of how to get to that vision. We assume you are interested in PLCs to help your school or district increase collegial learning, which in turn, will increase student learning. In Chapter 3 we outlined many of the specific policies, procedures, and organizational issues that need to be considered when integrating professional learning communities into the school's culture. We now turn to the process of preparing the initial steps for implementing PLCs.

Sir Isaac Newton's first law of motion says that bodies tend to stay at rest unless acted upon by an outside force. Organizations are no different—status quo is the natural state. It is easier to keep doing what we are doing rather than do something different. Overcoming status quo is neither easy nor quick. As a first step let's talk about what prevents action. Chris Argyris (1990) writes, "Human beings are not usually motivated to produce what they do not wish or intend" (p. xii). To prepare people in organizations to get involved in new learning and new processes, leaders must answer the question of "Why do anything different?" This requires clarity of outcomes and goals as well as answering the question of, "How does this affect me?" (Hall & Hord, 2006).

Beginning to implement is really working on a gap. The gap we are talking about is what Pfeffer and Sutton (2000) call the "knowing-doing gap." Our second question centers on how to close that gap. As with the Edmond's quote earlier, let's choose to make a difference. Let's remove or reduce the organizational barriers that prevent action. Closing the gap between what we say and what we do is another important step in making professional learning communities a reality. Thus, the question becomes, "Why aren't we implementing what we know is good practice?"

The decision to use data to inform our practice is another important step in preparing for professional learning communities. Educators will be meeting with their colleagues, engaging in real dialogue, and using their own data as a result of their work together. Southwest Educational Development Laboratory (Herbert, Murphy, Ramos, Vaden-Kiernan, & Buttram, 2006) completed a five-year study of low-performing schools. Staying focused on learning was one of the major goals. Facilitating conversations using student data was essential in determining what was working and what required changes. If, as the principal, you cannot help staff use data effectively, find someone who can. We believe staff members want to improve. They will use data to inform their professional practice, but they have to know how to do that. Principals and other leaders can provide training, professional development, and lead discussions about how data can be used to improve teaching practice.

As you think about initiating PLCs to increase conversations about learning among staff members, leaders will have to address the issues of change. Most people in organizations will be cautious about any change, and for good reason. Following are some questions to consider as you move toward implementing PLCs.

Why do we have to do anything differently?

If we know so much about what works, why is it we are not implementing what we know?

What does the principal do to keep the vision of a learning school at the center of attention?

This chapter focuses on what principals and other leaders do. Knowing why we are doing things differently is important. Knowing what to do is another extremely important element. Doing it, leading it, making it happen is the next step. Without action and follow-through, we have plans and dreams.

Why Do Things Differently?

From Peters (2003), comes this cryptic observation by General Eric Shinseki, Chief of Staff, U.S. Army: "If you don't like change, you're going to like irrelevance even less" (p. 3). Most of us in education have seen the results of change; however, we don't typically understand change since we do not look at change systemically. We usually view change through our narrow lens of how it affects us. First, our environment is changing, our clientele is changing, and our business is changing to a global environment. Business can respond to changing climates by outsourcing or importing workers from abroad or investing in new technology. Second, our schools are changing because of this and the increasing diversity of our students and community. More diversity in our schools requires a broader repertoire of teaching strategies. Students know more ways to learn than we know how to teach. The need for more strategies will continue into the foreseeable future. In one urban school, the diverse population included more than 10 percent new Somali students. That changes the school district responses to the new population of students.

A strategy we have used is to make the case for the future requirements for our students. Our students will live in a very different world than currently exists. Garreau (2005) writes that our future is in GRIN technologies: genetics, robotics, information, and nanotechnology. He further states that Duke University has an owl monkey that can move objects with her mind. University of California at Berkeley has developed an exoskeleton that allows people to lift 180 pounds like it was only 4.4 pounds. DARPA has developed a pill for chronic pain that will last for 30 days and the effects felt in 30 seconds. Neuroscientists are discovering new facts about the brain and how it functions. This emerging research on how the brain functions is sure to have implications for educators about effective teaching.

Here are some questions for you: How are you preparing the majority of our students to work in industries that focus on GRIN technologies? How are we preparing ourselves in order to teach students who will work in those industries? How do we organize our schools and districts to create stimulating environments that will help our teachers and administrators work with our students? This is what keeps us up at night. Are we preparing our students for the years 2015 or 2020? It will be a whole different world than exists today. Do you realize that the kindergarten class that begins school in the fall of 2007 will graduate in the year 2020? What will the world be like? What preparation will students need in order to survive and thrive in 2020? Are we prepared to prepare our young people?

Schools continue to struggle with these changes. However, as much as our environment and student population has changed, our schools and the way we conduct schools haven't changed very much.

The pressure to change is great. The question becomes what and how to change to make education better for students and adults and, ultimately, for society. We believe that our schools are getting better at teaching students, the strategies for teaching are increasing, and professional development is helpful. We also believe that the needs in the numbers of students, the requirements for postsecondary education, and skills for entry-level jobs in business are increasing at a faster rate than the school's ability to expand teaching strategies. We have slower feedback loops in education than in life after school. One of the outcomes we think schools must address is preparing students for life, not only for postsecondary schooling. We must address both. The gap between what is needed in the world and what we are able to deliver continues to widen.

First, let's start talking about the changes that are going on in schools and communities. By not talking about how we are changing, the message is that we don't change. Because the environment continues to change, we have to adapt. We are not necessarily changing our professional practice. We hear that educators don't want to change. We say, "Bullfeathers." Educators are changing all the time. The demographics of school districts continue to change. Poverty levels continue to increase, family structures are different than they were 30 years ago, and students are more mobile than before. Because the student populations are changing, the composition of communities is changing as well, and therefore the staff is changing.

Some questions are relevant here. How do we lead change? How do we know if how we are adapting is making a difference? How do we know what not to change? As student population changes, what worked in the past may not be working as well now.

Second, we believe change requires learning and learning requires changing your mind or readjusting how you perceive the world. Therefore, as a school, we will be learning continually with no end in sight. To deal with constant change, we believe there has to be continual learning. We didn't say this was going to be comfortable. As Neal Lane, science advisor to President Clinton, was quoted in *Shackleton's Way* (Morrell & Capparell, 2001):

Those organizations—be they businesses, schools, colleges and universities, government agencies—that prepare themselves for the unexpected and help to build a sense of community will, in my opinion, become the leaders in the twenty-first century. The same is true for each of us as individuals. (p. 8)

Commitment

Getting started requires a commitment to change the way we work. We will be more effective learning and changing if we are working in community. Working in community lets us understand differing points of view, provides more creativity, and includes more people in decisions. Learning with others requires humility and commitment. Making a commitment to someone else, especially a trusted colleague, is sometimes more effective than making a commitment to yourself. Being committed may be more important than being intelligent. Argyris (1990) noted the following:

Introducing the commitment model in a world dominated by the control model requires that important values and behavioral differences be resolved. The control model emphasizes short-term rewards, crisis orientation, quick fix, and covert evaluation. The commitment model emphasizes long-term rewards, problem-solving before crises arise, overt evaluations, and major responsibility for success on systems and groups. (p. 133)

The commitment model encourages staff to say what they know but might be afraid to say. It also allows people to advocate their principles, values, and beliefs in a way that invites inquiry. In other words, it increases both trust and commitment. There is a difference between merely contributing and making a commitment. When you think of bacon and eggs, the chicken makes a contribution, the pig makes full commitment.

New Statutes

Sometimes new legislation or policy decisions create the opportunity to start changing our professional practice. As an example of getting started, in Minnesota there is legislation that addresses new compensation plans for educators. The new alternative comp legislation is in two areas: evaluation and professional development. The statute citations are MS 122A.61 Subdivision 3(iii)(A) and Subdivision 4 and Subdivision 6. The Minnesota State Department of Education makes reference to working as a community of learners. Education Minnesota, the combined union (MFT) and the association (MEA) is looking at PLCs as one way to address the ongoing learning required for alternative compensation plans. In fact, Education Minnesota is offering PLC training for districts as they implement the alternative compensation package.

Some districts are using the phrase "collegial teams." We believe whatever they are called, professional learning communities offer a systematic way to enhance skills, share repertoire, and develop shared leadership. PLCs have the ability to enhance teacher quality, which, in turn, will increase student achievement.

The Knowing-Doing Gap

There are reasons that we do not put into practice what we know is right. For example, we know that "hands-on, activity-based" science classes increase knowledge retention. The reality is that with 37 students in a chemistry class, activity-based is not only hard but can be dangerous to organize. Another example is that detracking of classes has been shown to improve student achievement. The policy of tracking classes is probably more for political reasons than educational. Another example: Do we assign students to balance class size so that every student gets maximum time with the teacher, or do we assign classes based on parental pressure? This is a continuing question that administrators and teachers have to deal with based on the politics of the district. Some of these reasons should be addressed before the actual implementation begins; otherwise, progress may be limited and a false start can result in frustration.

More Than Knowing "What" to Do

One of the requirements needed to initiate and sustain PLCs will be knowing specifically what actions will be required of the professionals in the school or district. As Edmonds (1979) reminded us, we already know enough to make a difference for kids. Pfeffer and Sutton (2000) insist that knowing is not sufficient; we must also plan for action. One way to increase the chance of action is having action as part of the planning phase. For every conversation about planning a learning activity, ask the question of the group, "What behaviors or actions are you willing to take to implement our knowledge?" The sharing of specific actions can promote thinking, develop criteria for success, and support professional changes.

In addition to making action plans part of the planning and discussion, dedicate time for sharing of repertoire and reflecting on the results. We suggest being very clear about what was seen or heard that indicates success, failure, or a combination of both. Being able to talk about specific actions helps staff become clear about what a PLC looks like and sounds like. Determining the success indicators clarifies whether or not we obtained the desired results. Building the criteria ahead of time and talking about what is expected will increase credibility and clarity.

Talk Instead of Action

Another way to track our own effectiveness is to reflect on how much talk we do and ask the question, "Does our talk lead to action? If not, why not?" Meetings have been called the greatest time wasters. We call meetings that engage lengthy conversations but result in little or no action, which is an example of the "reverse butterfly effect." The *butterfly effect* means small changes can produce huge results. We know there are exceptions to this, but in our experience much talk has produced relatively little effect. There are examples of much fanfare, money, and time spent on programs that have shown few or no positive, long-lasting results. One of the ways we keep the knowing-doing gap alive is by substituting talk for action.

As you begin the process of starting professional learning communities, how will you and your colleagues support, require, encourage, and sustain action? The late Judy-Arin Krupp said, "Adults don't learn from the event; they learn from processing the event" (personal communication, 1984). We concur. What reflective processes do you have in place to increase the chance of learning from discussion and the implementation of ideas?

Past Practice

To initiate change, we must address the thoughts and concerns of staff members. "We have always done it this way here." "Once you have been here awhile, you will understand why we do it this way." This is what we heard when beginning our teaching careers. In some ways this is true and useful. There are practices that help organize and provide stability. There are also practices that get in the way or still exist even though the environment has changed. In order to get started, principals must discuss the results of current practice, how staff member learning contributes to school results, and the collaboration that can drive organizational improvement.

There is a story about cutting the ham in half. A daughter asked her mother why she cut the ham in half when cooking it for Easter dinner. The mother replied, "Because that is the way my mother did it." When the family got together for the dinner, the daughter asked grandmother why she cut the ham in half. The grandmother said that when she grew up on the farm, her mother had a wood-burning stove. The stove was small, so they had to cut the ham in half in order to get the ham into the oven. Sometimes we are still doing the same thing years later, even when the need has changed.

When we hear, "What person made that decision?" stop and think. That may have been the best decision given the available information at the time. Thank you for making the decision then. Now, as Bob Dylan's song "Things Have Changed" suggests, it is important to reevaluate decisions of the past from time to time. Reassessment keeps things current.

One of our favorite practices is to mine the minds of new people who come into the system. You can get information about the organization by asking new staff some questions like:

"What are you surprised by in this school?"

"What do you wish would have been explained to you before you started teaching?"

"What are the unspoken rules at this school?"

"Who has been the most helpful to you so far?"

"If you could start over, what is one thing you would change?"

If new employees trust you, they will tell you about the reality of your culture.

New staff members provide a perspective of the organization that is not available from those who have been there for a time. Ask your organization to listen, provide time for new people to speak, and honor their input. Everyone will learn a great deal. Newcomers will ask the naïve questions, "Why do you do this? Why do you do it this way? Is this what we are supposed to be doing?" That is a great opportunity for the system to learn. These questions from newer staff are gifts. Treat their questions as a gift, and learning will result.

Establishing trust will help get conversations started. Professional learning communities require trust to reach full benefits. The system has to be trustworthy for people to speak up. Experienced professionals might have to initiate the conversation in a thoughtful, nonthreatening, caring way. Tom Peters (2003) maintains that the chance of getting valuable information from our new people is inversely proportional to the chance of getting shot. In other words, if we nonverbally or verbally send the message, "Your question is stupid," "You are being uppity," or "We don't care," we won't get valuable unfiltered feedback. What an opportunity to miss!

Measurement Versus Good Judgment

Einstein once said, "Not everything that counts can be counted and not everything that can be counted counts." We do believe that assessment is possible and necessary; however, be careful not to rely only on what is easy to count. Knowing the numbers of people attending staff development gives you some data. Knowing if and how the professional learning has made an impact on teaching and learning would be more valuable. According to Killion (2002), knowing how professional learning impacts student achievement is the goal. If the staff is learning, students show more growth in achievement (Rosenholtz, 1989). True professional learning communities enable staff to learn.

So, what will you measure, assess, or evaluate that will tell you PLCs are making a difference? (This question is addressed in more detail in Chapter 6.) This question should be asked before PLCs get underway, or at least in the very early stages of implementation. The answer doesn't have to be perfect. As a matter of fact, we would guard against trying to find the perfect solution. Your system is unique. New questions will emerge. Treat them as learning opportunities, not as flies in the ointment.

Competition

Learning is not a race between professionals. Vygotsky (1986) opined that learning is social. We learn more in concert with others than alone. Consider how to bring professionals together socially as a way to begin learning together. This is a prime opportunity for professional development to help teachers and principals interact with one another prior to setting agendas. Sometimes getting started is getting people together. If the faculty is large, this step will be even more important. Do not assume all teachers know each other.

Keeping the vision on learning as opposed to who is learning the most is an important element of PLCs. One question to discuss is, How do we organize to share knowledge, skills, and applications throughout our school? Throughout the system? How can we make it easier to share? Getting together is one thing, facilitating knowledge and skills transfer is another important part. We must intentionally plan for transfer of knowledge and skills between professionals.

Focusing on Learning

In Chapter 1 we discussed the five characteristics of PLCs. These characteristics can be used by principals to encourage and sustain PLCs as part of the school culture. When we began our careers in education more than 35 years ago, we are sure we did not hear that continued learning was required. As a matter of fact the model was clear: Be good at math or science, learn the algorithms, and then demonstrate how you solve problems to the students. If you had the required content knowledge, you could teach.

Even when beginning administrative careers 30 years ago, we are sure no one told us that we would have to continue learning. Nor did we think we would be required to develop other leaders, to ensure we had succession leadership in schools and districts, and that both of those goals would be so important in the future. Principals are in a critical and unique position to develop this leadership and to help create professional learning communities. As we said early in this book, it takes other staff to be leaders alongside the principal.

Principals who talk more about learning and instruction for both staff and students create more professional dialogue. They work directly with staff and indirectly with students. Principals are the connection between the district and community to the school. Sometimes they must edit or modify what comes from above, but they are the link that makes things happen. As Chapter 1 mentioned, principals create the context for change to happen.

There is a Chinese proverb that states, "Sometimes you have to go slow in order to go fast." We are suggesting that the time spent listening, learning, and sharing repertoire will demonstrate results that far exceed each professional doing their own individual learning. Developing repertoire (having many ways to teach and solve problems) and flexibility (being able to use an array of strategies when you need them) can help less experienced professionals the most. When professionals share their talents and skills, they help the whole school develop a collective wisdom about learning and teaching. This takes time. That is not to say each professional doesn't have individual goals. Do we have the will to reclaim time to talk about learning in our schools for the individual and for the professionals as a community?

Murphy (2006) reminds us that the basis for leadership must be "learning, teaching and school improvement," not only crisis management and political issues. Sommers and Payne (2001) believe the principal has to have skills to deal with day-to-day issues in order to have time to focus on instruction. They go on to say that the principal who gets bogged down by minutia will not be able to spend time on learning and teaching. How do we keep learning, teaching, and improvement at the center of our schools? It takes leadership that is committed to keeping that focus. It takes teacher leadership to maintain that focus as well.

Hedgehog Concept

Collins (2005) declares one of the four areas of greatness is disciplined thought. One of the two suggestions for disciplined thought is the "Hedgehog Concept." Collins identifies hedgehogs as those who keep looking at the goal and don't get distracted, whereas those he calls "foxes" keep jumping around from one thing to another. Hedgehogs keep focused on making decisions with their most important values and vision in focus. Keeping the eyes, ears, head, and heart focused on learning is not easy, *and* it may be the most important thing we do.

Shared and Supportive Leadership

Teachers watch to see if what the principal says, "I believe in teaching and learning," is congruent with what he or she does, "actively engage in classroom instruction." As the principal teaches lessons in classes, observes and provides feedback for teaching staff, and promotes learning and teaching, the staff, students, and community believe what the leader says. The principal and other leaders get support from the staff and the staff gets support from their leaders. This reciprocal focus on teaching and learning is an important message to send.

We know a principal who regularly teaches class periods with or instead of teachers on leadership, thinking skills, and mathematics (where the principal is certified). This principal also teaches classes, through universities, to the staff for graduate credit. Parents have also enrolled in these classes. The principal speaks at community service organizations, other schools in the district, and at professional conferences.

Staff members tend to share responsibility when leaders are more involved in the day-to-day practice of learning. Coteaching with staff members is an excellent way to model for staff and students.

Teaching

At one high school we worked with, the parent organization wanted to bring in speakers on learning at least once every other month. On one of the months the principal presented information on adolescent brain research that was helpful to the parents. This modeled the principal as a learner and a teacher. Other topics presented by the principal and other teacher leaders included social and emotional development, dealing with teenagers about conflict, chemical abuse, and communication skills. Parents told other parents, and the numbers who attended increased dramatically over the years.

As principal you can teach classes. In a student leadership class, organized by the student council advisor, a principal taught four class periods during the term on leadership, learning styles, and collaboration. This provided firsthand knowledge to student leaders, gave an opportunity for the principal to teach, and provided the principal with direct feedback from students. As student issues surfaced during the year, conversations shifted from the hard conflict of "What I want is . . . " to "How can we come up with a solution to. . . . " We have found teaching classes is the quickest way to tell students and staff that you are interested in learning and teaching. This can be a humbling experience as well. Having sweaty palms in front of 30 moving targets isn't easy, but it is important.

Humility

We believe that in any theory of learning and change there must be an element of humility present. In other words, if you already know the answer, can you learn anything new? Does your school culture encourage or inhibit questions? How do we treat people who ask the tough questions? Faculty meetings, staff lounges, and committee work can be a barometer of how learning-ready the culture is within the school.

Some of these examples are about principal voice. The principal's voice must be clear about the vision, must promote and encourage learning, and must find every opportunity to enhance the learning culture. The principal is the primary model of what the vision is and can be for staff and students. What the principal does, where time is spent is more important than what the principal says. If the principal does not model a desired behavior, it is unlikely it will be manifested in the culture.

Connections

The school is not an island. Surrounding the principal and other leaders is a support system that includes the central office, the super-intendent, school boards, and other ancillary positions in the district. How connections are made to the learning goal with the other groups can provide strong messages about collegial learning and improving student learning.

A school district in Ohio is one example of a connected staff that is focused on learning. This district had regular meetings with its cus-todial and food services staffs. The custodial staff were focused on repairing and cleaning because they knew this led to an environment more conducive for learning for the students. The food service staff would say they were serving nutritious food to fuel learning. Another example is a California assistant superintendent whom we recently talked with. He asked the principal, "What can I do that will make this school better for kids' learning?"

Collective Learning and Its Application

We suggest that both actions and words are critical in leading professional learning communities. As leaders, we have to speak our truth about learning. We have to speak about what we believe. Speaking clearly increases our own learning, the learning among staff members, and ultimately increases student learning. When we speak clearly, community members can understand us better, and they may be more willing to share their truths with us. There are many oppor-tunities to keep learning on the front of the agenda. Is learning part of the dialogue in every professional meeting? Principals who spend time with staff in committees and meetings and talk about learning—their learning and student learning—build learning communities. In classes, principals can teach lessons, ask staff what they are learning about teaching, and ask students about what is effective learning.

Including Students

Students continue to be an untapped resource in many ways. There are schools where student opinion about learning is used as feedback. A high school principal we know convened a meeting with 85 ninth grade students to get input on how to reduce the dropout rate. After a day of dialogue, asking specific questions, and receiving honest feedback, a new school-within-a-school was implemented the following year. Those students became mentors for the incoming ninth grade students the next year. At one school we visited, students take a pretest on their own before taking the final evaluation over the chapter. The student and the teacher identify areas that need more work using the results of the pretest. The teacher makes changes in the lesson using the cumulative results of the pretests. If patterns develop and show many students having difficulty, the instructor will redesign the lesson. Those teachers find useful ways to engage students in assessing their learning.

Taking Action

How do we develop new norms in meetings? One way might be to start with a quote about learning or leadership. Another way is to set the meeting up with a story, a video clip, or professional learning activities to engage people's minds. Whatever the strategy, it can be linked to the learning content and context of the school or district. Professional learning communities continually learn together both content and process. Sometimes it is valuable for the members to share what have been great learning experiences for them. What made it so powerful? Was it about a person, the process, or both?

Modeling

As we've said, the principal is the primary learning model. Other leaders in school can be as important for modeling learning. Like the four-year-old in the story of the wooden bowl, who sees how his parents treat his elderly grandfather, forcing him to eat from a wooden bowl instead of china (Olsen & Sommers, 2004), staff watch to see what the leader is doing, where he or she spends time, and what he or she talks about. It is important that the principal's voice is heard talking about learning. It is equally important that teachers' voices are heard talking about learning. The more staff members who talk about learning, the more learning becomes the centerpiece of our vision, mission, and values. Whatever the topic the PLC is discussing, the principal contributes to that learning with their staff members as colleagues.

The emerging research concerning mirror neurons give physiological support to what we only understood as modeling. The mirror neurons in the prefrontal cortex actual fire together when watching someone else do an activity. It is as if they are doing it themselves. Modeling initiates neural pathways that if strengthened will help anchor new behaviors. Modeling, indeed, may be the quickest way to teach.

Supportive Conditions

According to McLaughlin & Phillips (1991) and Susan Rosenholtz (1989), the quality of the professional community that exists in schools seems more critical to the integrity of teaching and learning for teachers and students than any other characteristic. This idea may represent one of the most important factors of the workplace. We know that collective action may be more important than the action planned. Many faculties have had lots of training on different models of curriculum and instruction. Those faculties who can come together to build consensus, agree upon the actions required, and follow through with implementation show better results than a collection of diverse goals. Again, as Collins (2005) states, leaders must get agreement on the frameworks we use and remain flexible on how to reach the goals.

The reality of schools is that isolation has been the norm. Typically the teachers have been in their classrooms, with their students, responsible for what happens during the day, the month, the year. Professional learning communities are a change of habit and expectations: PLCs suggest we work together in new ways for the advancement of everyone. Working together has not been the normal way we operate. Let's face it, it is easier to do your own thing on your own time. We have worked with schools where the culture allowed staff to do what they wanted in their classrooms. For teachers, this is much like being self-employed. One downside of such independence or individuality is that the staff's selective enforcement of policies, regulations, or ideas confuses students. One question we sometimes ask is, "Is your need to be an individual stronger than the need to collaborate for the good of the whole?" If the need for individualization is strong for everyone, collaboration will suffer. The results of student performance also are reduced, since there are few agreed-upon standards.

Saint Augustine said:

In essentials, we need unity.
In non-essentials we need flexibility.
In everything we need charity.

Shared Personal Practice

When staff members operate as individuals, there is limited transfer of knowledge within the school. Staff members who stay disconnected and in their own rooms reduce the shared repertoire. To improve we must keep learning from each others' experiences. Certainly we each learn in our individual and in our collective ways at the same time. Unless we engage in conversation with others, we are limited by our own thinking and at our own level of consciousness.

Bandura (1997) has written about four stages of learning. When staff members are not conscious about their professional practice, they have difficulty talking about and specifically changing their ideas. Being conscious of behavior is a prerequisite for improvement. A person will go from unconscious incompetence (not knowing we don't know), to conscious incompetence (knowing we don't know), to conscious competence (knowing we know), to unconscious competence (not knowing we know). As we move through these stages when we learn new knowledge or skills, we are reminded that issues must be in the consciousness for us to examine our policies, practices, and possible barriers. As long as we remain unconscious, we will not change how we teach or lead. We want to be aware of what is happening and remain open to finding new ways of solving problems.

Consciousness

Some of the best teachers perform seamlessly in the classroom. Unless they can be conscious of their thinking and behavior, it is difficult to change actions. When in dialogue with others, the process of dialogue creates conversations that share information. Sharing what works among professionals accelerates group learning, creates new possibilities, and develops communities of practice. Wenger (1998) states that sharing repertoire among professionals builds stronger learning communities.

Creativity

Einstein was quoted as saying; "You cannot solve problems with the same level of thinking that got you into them." When professionals get a chance to problem solve with each other, the collective solutions are far better for more people than they would be with each person solving their own problems. Sharing creative strategies increases the collective learning among the adults in the school.

Coaching

The practice of peer coaching is a great asset in sharing personal practice. When professionals are able to get into each other's classrooms, when administrators observe other administrators, and when educational assistants get to learn from each other, the system learns. Coaching conversations enhance personal practice in schools and help us to apply what we know. Increasing the learning conversations in the school helps everyone to become more effective. When staff members learn, schools learn. When schools learn, students learn. This is an interdependent collective learning process.

An example of coaching happened when we were having a dialogue with a veteran teacher. We asked a question, "What will the students be doing while you are teaching this concept?" The veteran teacher responded after about a minute of thinking, "I never thought of what the students will be doing, I have spent all my years thinking about what I will be doing." Coaching questions have the ability to help shift the thinking and the actions in classrooms and in the school. The other staff that witnessed this process started to increase the focus on student behavior as a result of this conversation.

Keeping the Focus and Continuing to Learn

How do we keep the focus on learning and create the conditions so that ongoing learning is the cultural norm, not the exception? This is a great question that takes perseverance on the part of leaders and staff. A leader can lead *and* we want other professionals to lead as well. Sharing leadership with teachers in the school will help demonstrate that learning is everybody's business. One of the first steps in building the capacity for learning is a ruthless assessment of reality. Having courage to tell the truth without blame or judgment is required for accurate assessments. A beginning step can be looking at student data. Which students are not performing at the level required? What interventions have we tried? What are new ways for teachers to teach struggling students? This can be uncomfortable as educators know relationships are important. Telling the truth and looking at data may be uncomfortable. We suggest the strongest organizations have the courage to tell the truth, put all data and ideas on the table, and are transparent in their decision-making process.

Current State of Affairs

A superintendent told us once that he didn't understand why we always wanted to know what wasn't working. Our response was that people are sitting on their own disaster fantasies. They have experiences of what hasn't worked in the past. We have found getting issues on the table enables the group to deal with some of the issues directly and sets the tone that everything is open. Open learning organizations do not hide; they are transparent and have open access to information (Chapter 3). Parking lot conversations that take place after meeting together are not helpful: These are the conversations that do not include all players, that are "behind-the-back" conversations. Miscommunication, false assumptions, and hurt feelings can result.

There are schools at which staff members have not worked collaboratively in the past. If collaboration has not been the norm, a principal will have to find ways to get staff to know each other. One principal whom we know set up chairs in the parking lot for the staff meeting. This was a way to say, "Let's have one meeting." The principal told the staff that he didn't want to waste time. He said, "Let's not have two meetings, the one in the library and one in the parking lot." This was an extreme example of getting the faculty to come together and discuss all issues openly and more honestly.

After knowing what currently exists, discuss what our future is if nothing changes. What is our future if we do change? It is one thing to complain about something, quite another to do something. It takes no courage to chronically complain. There should be no more awards for time telling; awards are for those who build better clocks.

Everyone Contributes

Another way to begin professional learning communities is by sharing data and talking about how to respond to the results. This helps staff members take responsibility for the results we are getting at the school level. We want to discuss what our contribution is in keeping the system where it is and what our contribution is for making it better. A minister in Minneapolis told us once, "When ignorance ends, responsibility begins." That is a powerful statement. So, personally and as a group, what is our contribution to the current state and what is our contribution for creating something different?

Collecting and Using Data

To continue learning, what processes are in place to keep conversations going, increasing trust and positive relationships, and sharing repertoire throughout the school? How will we know we are closing the knowing-doing gap? What data will we collect? How will we use the data collected? How does data become information that informs us?

How do we transform information into knowledge that can help us anticipate outcomes? How will knowledge become wisdom so we know when and when not to use specific practices? Each person alone can answer these questions. However, greater thinking and creating a system together are by-products of doing this in community. Another result of learning in community is identification of multiple ideas and information sources. In one district we know a principal started by identifying the in-house experts who were already on the faculty. The principal knew that many teachers had attended professional learning workshops. Collecting the names and area of expertise helped the staff members know who could be a resource in the school on specific topics. Many times we go outside for the exact knowledge and skills that reside next door or down the hall. Professional educators have a tremendous storehouse of knowledge that they can share.

The process of reflection can help stimulate conversations that allow us to reflect on what we are doing, what results we are getting, and how we might do things differently. We recommend keeping this reflective process as an ongoing dialogue. Research shows more success is tied to reflection—it helps us make better decisions (Argyris & Schön, 1978; Perkins, 2003; Schön, 1983). Reflection includes planning ahead, creating possible goals and scenarios that can accomplish those goals, and reviewing previous events. Most of us know about reflecting back on a lesson, a presentation, or an event. If we reflect, decide what went right, and what we would change, we usually make better decisions the next time. Without reflection, we tend to do what we have always done in the past. So how do we keep reflective practice alive for what the National Staff Development Council calls ongoing, job-embedded, and results-driven professional learning in our schools?

To initiate professional learning communities successfully, there will have to be time dedicated for teachers to meet. *Ongoing* means keeping the conversation going daily, weekly, and monthly. *Job-embedded* refers to making conversation relevant to what teaching and learning requires. Job-embedded can also mean to use in-house expertise. Every school has resident experts. *Results-driven* certainly suggests using data. It also means to talk about how we will know we are getting closer to our goals or farther away. What are the indicators that are going to tell us? It is really like driving a car. How do you know you are getting closer to your destination? Most of us look at road signs. What are the road signs you and your colleagues are looking at that inform you about your status?

Building the capacity to talk about real issues, in a trusting place, with other committed professionals is powerful. Build the case, set the context for *why,* and then create the professional learning community for the *how.* There is an acronym in 12-step programs, like Alcoholics Anonymous, for *how.* The *how* stands for *h*onesty, *o*penness, and *w*illingness. Pretty good advice.

Leadership Implications

Here are some suggestions for initiating and sustaining the professional learning community.

1. *Ask* why *before* how. Principals and other leaders should engage their staff in discussing why we should start PLCs, what our school would accomplish, and what this means to each member for their own learning before getting into the details.

2. *Learn and teach others.* By being part of a learning group, the principal is modeling expectations of the staff. Bring ideas, articles, and creative teaching processes to contribute and teach others. Lead by modeling. Be the head "learner."

3. *Action counts more than plans.* As leader you want small quick wins, so take action. As momentum builds, the staff will implement actions with greater influence. If you can be transparent about what you are learning about learning, teaching, and leading, this will be leading by example. This can be one of the most valuable things you do. To quote Stevie Ray, an improvisation teacher in Minneapolis, "Teams thrive on momentum, not accuracy."

4. *Be kind to yourself.* Normally there is no learning without mistakes. Remember Thomas Edison found 1,800 ways *not* to build a light bulb. Farson and Keyes (2002) titled their book *The One Who Makes the Most Mistakes, Wins.* It is okay to make mistakes. We just don't want to make the same mistakes. There is ample opportunity to make different mistakes, thereby moving learning ahead.

5. *Reduce fear.* W. Edwards Deming noted years ago that we should drive fear out of the organization. Fear limits learning. We know this from organizational development literature and the emerging brain research. We can help build trust and reduce fear by having norms of accepting ideas, accepting the people who tell their ideas,

and not rushing to judgment too quickly. Accepting diversity of thought can be a precondition to accepting diverse groups.

6. *Beware of the prophet who carries one book.* We have been in education a long time, and we like this Yiddish proverb. We do not know of any book, including this one, that has all the answers. We can use books, literature, and PLC programs that are already underway as great sources of information. You as a leader, with the other learning leaders in your school, will collaborate with all staff to translate ideas into action in your own school.

7. *Beware of false analogies.* Collins, in *Good to Great and the Social Sector* (2005), pronounced that business does not have the answer. Business has some useful information and mental models. Schools also have lots of knowledge and some good mental models. But schools have to look to themselves to generate answers for their schools. We can use research and past history to guide us, but we have to do it ourselves.

8. *Measure what matters.* How do we know we are making a difference? Are the things we are measuring giving us the right information to inform our practice?

9. *Remember they are watching.* Everyone in the school will be watching what the principal does, not listening to what he or she says. Actions do speak louder than words, and leadership is demonstrated by where you spend your time and the actions you are taking on a daily basis.

Vignette

Beginning to Change the Way We Do Business

As a principal, you can't create time. We all wish we could. So, if you can't create time, can you rearrange time? This is one way to shift the culture and increase staff learning. In two high schools, a principal we know did two things. The principal went to the union president to find out if the teachers would support a redistribution of time. In other words, would they support the idea of taking a day off in March (which would make another three-day weekend, students were already off) and replace that with an additional hour of meetings each month connected to faculty meetings? Both times the answer was, "Yes." The principal said they would not force anyone to change if they really didn't want to *and* they wanted at least a 70 percent vote among the staff in order to change the professional development schedule.

Then the principal went to the superintendent to ask if she would have a problem with this change in time schedule if the staff agreed. The superintendent was very nervous. So, the principal reframed the issue as a pilot program that would be evaluated at the end of the year (the next year the other schools wanted the same change).

The principal went in front of the faculty to explain the plan. Seventy percent would have to vote "Yes" to try it. Those not wanting it would continue with the scheduled staff development day. The new plan would have teachers' input into what they would study. They would run the regularly scheduled Tuesday afternoon meetings, with makeup meetings (for staff who missed because of coaches', advisors', doctors' appointments, and such) the following Wednesday morning. The first school voted 71 percent and second school voted 93 percent.

The rest of the story was that only two teachers in the first school and only one in the second school chose not to join the professional learning communities that we established. Did those teachers do staff development in March of that year? You bet your sweet bippy they did. As principal you must follow through. The professional development committee and the principal planned a day for those not attending PLCs, and they delivered the day of training.

The point is that there are creative ways to rearrange time. One of the major jobs of the principal is to arrange time for staff to talk to each other in order to get started. In *Communities of Practice,* Wenger (1998) advises that one of the elements of creating these communities is planning for mutual engagement of the participants. They have to get in the same room to have dialogue. The other two elements are (1) making sure people can talk together, not do parallel conversations, and (2) sharing repertoire. We want professionals to share what they know, what they are learning, and what they value. All of this takes trust. Trust is the social glue that provides the basis for trying new ideas. Trust also gives principals permission to suggest and implement professional learning communities. Without trust, not much will happen in the short term or the long term.

At the end of the year, we evaluated the process. In both schools there was unanimous approval to continue the professional learning communities. Other schools in both districts adopted a similar schedule. Rearranging time, making sure professionals get to talk to each other about students and instruction (topics that matter), and helping transfer knowledge throughout the system are valuable processes for a learning organization.

Rocks in the Road

One of the rocks you may encounter is being in overload with many different initiatives. Keeping the focus on PLCs, their operation, and monitoring PLC results will be a major accomplishment. The suggestions presented all have potential rocks. For example, an educator's tendency is to develop elaborate plans on how to implement a policy. Sometimes the goal gets lost in the specific steps. Yes, the devil is in the details, and the leader must make sure the staff continues to focus on the goal. Leaders should not let the specific details override the learning goals of the PLC.

Another source of rocks is the question of "How do we do this?" From our experience, if you get mired in the *how* of the program before discussing the *why*, the details may overwhelm good people. A resource for this is Block (2003), *The Answer to How Is Yes.* The author suggests reframing a question like, "How do others do this?" to "What are we willing to create for ourselves?" Another question is, "How long is this going to take?" Block suggests reframing the question as, "What are we willing to commit to make this happen?" Reframing can be a useful strategy to eliminate or step around the rocks in the road.

Engage in Learning Activities

Compare and contrast your organization to the following story.

> A group of frogs were traveling through the woods, and two of them fell into a deep pit. All the other frogs gathered around the pit. When they saw how deep the pit was, they told the two frogs that they were as good as dead. The two frogs ignored the comments and tried to jump up out of the pit with all of their might. The other frogs kept telling them to stop, that they were as good as dead. Finally, one of the frogs took heed to what the other frogs were saying and gave up. He fell down and died. The other frog continued to jump as hard as he could. Once again, the crowd of frogs yelled at him to stop the pain and just die. He jumped even harder and finally made it out. When he got out, the other frogs said, "Did you not hear us?" The frog explained to them that he was deaf. He thought they were encouraging him the entire time.

This story teaches two lessons:

1. There is power of life and death in the tongue. An encouraging word to someone who is down can lift them up and help them make it through the day.

2. A destructive word to someone who is down can be what it takes to kill them. Be careful of what you say.

Speak life to those who cross your path. The power of words . . . it is sometimes hard to understand that an encouraging word can go such a long way. Anyone can speak words that tend to rob another of the spirit to continue in difficult times. Special is the individual who will take the time to encourage another. Be special to others.

What are three or more actions you could take to support people and ideas at your school?

During the vacation or trip, do we know how to act? We have the knowledge, and we must take action. Most of us listen to people around us when we are in a new environment. By listening, we gain lots of information. We also observe people around us. By watching, we learn new customs, rules, and mores. We develop the skills to behave appropriately.

Another way we learn about new surroundings is by questions. If we don't know, we ask someone. If we get into trouble and problems arise, we use our mediation skills and try to resolve the conflict.

We try to be alert to the nuances of new territory. There is always something to learn when in a new place. After we have experienced the new culture, most of us start acting like we are natives. We do as others do. We also want to retain our own culture and knowledge from previous experience. Staying open to new possibilities is difficult but necessary to gain from our travels.

5

What Are the Skills Needed to Lead Professional Learning Communities?

Organizations are made of conversations.

Ernesto Gore

You cannot order people to become cohesive. You cannot order great performance. You have to create the culture and climate that makes it possible. You have to build the bonds of trust.

Michael Abrashoff

Trust is the building block of the organization.

Margaret Wheatley

In the previous chapters we have discussed what professional learning communities (PLCs) are, why they are important, and the leadership imperative to make them operate successfully. We also examined the structures, policies, and procedures that are required as well as some initial steps for getting started. We now turn our attention to some of the skills that will enhance and sustain our learning community and its organizational culture.

Larraine Matusak, a senior scholar at the University of Maryland's James MacGregor Burns Academy of Leadership, exhorts us, "Every day of your life is filled with opportunities to be creative, to act with purpose and potency. You don't need an elevated position or a title of great importance to assume a leadership role." While it is true that you don't need a position to be a leader, the principal is the identified leader to focus the conversation and the behaviors in the school that will initiate and sustain learning.

In this chapter, we address essential skills required for successful professional learning communities by answering the following questions:

> What skills contribute to meaningful conversations that promote professional learning communities?

> How do we encourage, enhance, and sustain reflective practice as a part of, not separate from, our daily work?

> How do we manage conflict to increase learning rather than letting conflict decrease our capacity?

The critical skills needed to foster meaningful conversations, encourage, enhance, and sustain reflective practice, and manage conflict should be adopted and promoted by all school leaders and used in the day-to-day activities of the school. Just as modeling is the first way students learn from adults, the same is true for adults. The adults, the professionals in the school, need models for what is expected.

Conversational Skills to Promote Professional Learning Communities

Conversational skills are the first skills the principal must develop among staff members to encourage, enhance, and sustain professional learning communities. We discuss several conversation modes here. Isaacs (1999) makes the distinction between discussion and dialogue. *Discussion* comes from the same root word as *percussion* and *concussion.* The analogy is beating on or continuing to drum on the same issue. *Discussion* could lead to debate that is a win/lose contest, but we also use discussion to make decisions. The point is to engage in the skill that is aligned with the desired outcome.

The dialogue concept, according to Isaacs (1999), Bohm (1989), and Garmston and Wellman (1999), promotes meaning and understanding among the participants. Therefore, in dialogue, meaning is clarified through the interchange of ideas. Carse (1986) discusses finite games like gin rummy, Monopoly™, and Sorry, which have a goal of winning. When someone wins, the game is over. Carse describes infinite games as those where the goal of the game is to continue the game. Therefore, dialogue is used to create infinite conversations to promote learning for the adults. We contend that professional learning communities should use such an infinite process to maximize learning in schools. Maximizing learning for the adults will maximize learning for the students.

To successfully employ dialogue, we must actively listen to others, suspend judgment, and resist premature closure. The term "Zeigarnick Effect" is used in the literature (Cooper & Sawaf, 1996, p. 102) to describe groups rushing to an answer too quickly without giving enough think time or to consider multiple options.

Listening

There are many sources and references in the literature about listening. Burley-Allen (1995) notes that in communicating we spend 9 percent of our time writing, 16 percent of our time reading, 35 percent of our time speaking, and 40 percent of our time listening. So, we ask, where do we teach listening in schools? How do we teach listening skills to the adults? How do we practice active listening in our professional learning communities?

The Art of Cognitive Coaching (Costa & Garmston, 2002) describes behaviors that are barriers to good listening. Costa and Garmston mention three barriers. Autobiographical barriers occur when we hear the other person talking and we are waiting to tell what happened to us instead of focusing on what is being said. The second barrier occurs when there are questions that pop into our heads. We hear the other person talking, and instead of listening we are formulating our next question. The third barrier arises when we start by listening, but we quickly focus on the solution the other person should do to solve the problem. All three of these behaviors can interrupt active listening.

We sometimes ask this question in workshops: "How much of your time is spent waiting and how much of your time is spent listening?" We suggest you track your own behavior for a week and see how much time you spend really listening to the other person and how much time you are spending in one of the three barriers mentioned.

Setting Aside Judgment

Another major challenge to sustaining ongoing conversations is setting aside judgment in order to stay open to different points of view and new ideas. It is easy to filter information, stories, and other people's point of view through our own lens. It is quite another to set aside judgment to get full meaning. This is difficult work. Think of a time when you felt judged by someone. Did that promote your own thinking or shut thinking down? Did you feel listened to or patronized?

We are not saying that you should never judge someone or an idea. As a matter of fact, teachers and administrators are paid to judge others: their performance, their abilities, and their products. However, judgment can be either praise or punishment, both of which can shut down thinking. Praise sends the message the answer is right, so the brain stops searching for the answer. Judgment stops thinking because the amygdala, the emotional center, stops the neocortex. (For additional information, see Kohn, 1993; Deci, 1995; and Wolfe, 2001.) To promote thinking, diversity of thought, and extending infinite conversations, we recommend setting aside judgment and considering alternative ideas.

Questions

We recommend two practices related to questioning for principals and other leaders. First, think of a question that might provide clarity. Many times an idea that initially does not seem to have merit is being suggested based on someone's personal or professional perspective. By asking a clarifying question, without judgment, you may uncover a great idea or a point of view that is unknown by the group. An example of how thinking can get shut down by judgment happened when a few teachers said the evaluation system was not working. We could have responded by saying, "That is the contract, that is the procedure, end of story." But when we asked, "What would be a better option to the way we do things with evaluation?" The response by staff members suggested they wanted to learn in groups. This led to a pilot program of a professional development process as an alternative to the perfunctory evaluation system. It was amazing how the staff was ready to learn, and the principal opened the possibility for developing a whole new accountability system that was focused on learning.

Observations

Another way to respond is expressed in Dennis Sparks's book, *Leading for Results* (2005). Sparks suggests we can state our observations, what is true for us, without blame or judgment. Carol Sanford, in her article published in *Organizational Dynamics*, states that feedback is useful under two conditions: nonjudgmental data and nonjudgmental inquiry. Judgment is evaluation and is necessary in managing organizations and people. Leaders have to make decisions, which involves making a judgment of what is right or what is the best alternative. When trying to increase learning, judgment often shuts down thinking. Kohn (1993), Deci (1995), and others have written extensively on the power of judgment, both positive and negative.

When we are trying to create learning cultures and develop strategies to strengthen PLCs, we must be very careful on how we use judgment, and the majority of time stay with inquiry.

Think for a moment how you react to judgment and how you react to questions. How do you react when I ask, "What mistakes do you plan not to repeat?" First, you are focused on figuring out what the mistakes were. Second, you start focusing on what I, as the supervisor, think are the mistakes. Then, you probably think about what is the safest answer that will end the conversation.

However, if I ask, "As you think about the results you got in this lesson, how, if at all, would you change it next time?" Now the person is responding to a question. The brain tends to think of more ways to respond, without fear. Language matters. Individual and group thinking can be enhanced by how we ask questions or make judgments. There are times to use both. Leaders must have both skills available to them. It is not to be adversarial; it is to make sure thoughts, experiences, and suggestions get heard. When we state observations with blame, judgment, or our own spin, we usually get a negative or defensive response. We want responses to be different from putting up barriers to stop possible learning. We want observations to promote thinking and expand possibilities for teachers and administrators.

In addition to active listening and suspending judgment, staying open-minded for a designated time before making a decision can allow new solutions. In our fast-paced work of education, we are all under pressure to make decisions and make them quickly. When there were gunshots outside our school, we did not say, "Gee, I wonder if that is a Remington or Winchester shotgun?" We hit the deck. However, learning takes time and is messy. Messy problems usually don't have quick answers. From our experience, quick answers sometimes have intended consequences. They usually have unintended consequences.

Staying Open

So, the question is how does a principal, staff member, or community member stay open-minded long enough to get enough input, suggestions, and points of view from many different sources before making a final judgment? One strategy is to make sure you have all points of view in the room. This means everyone has a chance to speak on a topic and to allow his or her voice to be heard. That means we actively invite people with different perspectives or different backgrounds. Sometimes the naysayer is the harbinger of problems that are formidable. Listen to them; it may save you time later on. We also believe you must invite those who tend to be quiet and reflective. Sometimes the one who does not speak up in groups might have the answer or at least part of the answer. Get as many of them as possible at the table to hear multiple points of view before a decision is made. This will take more time and be a messier process because there are more people at the table and more issues to be addressed; in short the process is more complex but can yield better decisions.

Staying open in a time-pressured environment like school is not easy. It takes courage from the principal and other leaders to let the thinking, planning, and reflecting process take its course. As stated earlier, premature closure on an idea can limit a thoughtful approach. Not making decisions can reduce the capacity to act in schools. It is a delicate balance at times. This is exactly why we need established norms for dialogue, including balancing advocacy and inquiry, balancing input with decision making, and balancing the capacity to act with reflective thought. Leaders sometimes have to step forward and make decisions. Leaders must also try to make sure people's views are heard and taken seriously.

What Is the Goal?

There is one last conversational element that is important to remember. What do you want? What is the goal? Scott (2002) maintains that most people have absolute clarity about what they don't want. Your goal, as a leader, is to help yourself and others to define what they do want—in other words, clarify the goal. Sometimes you have to restate the goal several times in different ways. Restating adds clarity and gives a chance for others to speak about what it means to them. Your ability to shift the conversation from what people don't want to what they do want is critical to the conversation and to taking effective action.

From our experience, if we can't move the conversation to what we want, a lot of wasted time and energy is spent in unproductive dialogue and discussion. Being able to move the conversation involves listening: Does the conversation focus on the existing state? If so, normally the language is defensive in nature and about what we can't do or can't change. Once you move the conversation to what we *do* want, you will notice a change in energy and language. The language becomes more constructive, creating possibilities about how to get to the desired state, and the energy level of the conversation is higher. So, what do you want and how are you going to get there?

Embedding Reflective Practice in Our Daily Work

The questions "What do you want?" and "How are you going to get there?" are examples of reflective questions. Reflection causes people to think about what is happening or is going to happen in classrooms, schools, districts, and so on. There are different kinds of reflection. York-Barr, Sommers, Ghere, and Montie (2006) describe four kinds of reflection.

Reflection on Action

Reflection on action is what most of us think about. It is reflecting back on something that has happened. In professional learning communities, educators use the results of their work to reflect back on what they did, what they might do differently next time to get different results, and start to assess patterns in their teaching practice. This takes time, but research suggests reflection improves instruction and student achievement.

Questions for reflecting on action may include:

- How did the lesson go?
- Did you get the results you were hoping for? Why or why not?
- Compare and contrast what you did with what you had planned.

- What patterns or themes are emerging from your teaching?
- What might you do differently next time?
- What do you want to make sure you do next time?

Collecting data, analyzing data, and using data to inform teaching practice is an example of reflecting on our actions. Having dialogue about data, what to collect, how to collect it, and how to use it is an important assessment process to be used in professional learning communities. The question becomes, "How do you know you are getting the outcomes you want?" (Please see Chapter 6.)

Reflection for Action

A second type of reflection is reflecting for action. This means we reflect forward, planning how to find ways to teach better, develop solutions for problem areas, and so on. Reflecting forward is a major component of professional learning communities because it helps us to develop goals, procedures, and ways to measure success. The ability to plan with a team, determine success indicators, and develop measures of success are critical steps for the staff to be conscious of in their teaching practice.

Questions for reflecting for action may include:

- What are some of the goals you have in mind?
- When you are successful, what will you see the students doing or hear them saying?
- What are some of the possible ways that you are going to teach this lesson or concept?
- What data might you collect to tell you the strategy is working?

Reflection in Action

Third, there is reflection in action. This occurs when we are actually teaching. It is in the moment. It is the voice in the head that says, "This isn't working and I don't have a plan B." We do not address this kind of reflection very often in professional learning communities. Based on Klein's (1998) work on mental simulation and pattern recognition, it may be a worthwhile topic for discussion. Reflection in action is also called "situational awareness," to which Marzano, Waters, and McNulty (2005) refer in the meta-analysis on leadership.

A principal, reflecting on what he does during the school day, once said, "My job is improvisation. I never need a to-do list, I just show up and people tell me what to do." Because of the hectic pace of the school day, and in fact, the world, that is what many principals and other leaders end up doing during the day when they are in action. Fortunately, we can learn skills to deal with the frenzied pace of improvisation. Mary Catherine Bateson (1989) wrote a book titled *Composing a Life.* One of her philosophies was, "Life is improvisation." This principal agreed with that sentiment.

He decided that if his professional life was improvisation, he had better get better at it. So, he went off to a comedy club to take improvisation classes. During the first session, within the first 15 minutes, the instructor had 19 people who did not know each other working together in teams. The principal was amazed at how quickly teams could work together for a common goal. Since that time the principal took several sets of classes and started teaching improvisation as part of leadership preparation classes and staff development presentations.

This principal also brought the improvisation teacher into schools and district offices to teach communication skills, teamwork, and conflict management strategies using improvisation techniques. One way to get better at reflection in action is to use and practice improvisation techniques. It will build confidence and competence.

Staff members like to talk to other staff about what goes on in their head while they are teaching. We think most of us like to know we are not that different from others, and sharing that information builds trust.

Reflecting Within

Last, there is reflection "within," which happens in those quiet moments in our life when we have time to think by ourselves. This doesn't happen much in schools, where constant motion is the norm. We wholly support reflecting within, but that usually will happen singly and not in communities.

Another resource for the process of reflection for personal insights is the work of Parker Palmer, *Courage to Teach* (1998). Palmer teaches a process to develop skills and attitudes for creating a trustworthy organization in which teachers can grow both personally and professionally. Palmer wants to reignite teachers' passion for learning and teaching. Most teachers come into the profession wanting to make a difference for students. Through professional learning communities, we can help keep that as one of the goals for teachers and principals. Making a difference for students is at the heart of teaching and of PLCs.

Walk-Throughs

Publications that discuss walk-throughs and professional development around walk-throughs for principals and administrators are abundant. The concept of getting principals into classrooms is a good one and should be encouraged. The more principals are in classrooms, the signal is clear: Learning and instruction are primary goals.

We have a word of caution, however. If the walk-throughs become a perfunctory, four- to five-minute visit, with a slip of paper handed to the teacher and no follow-up conversation, we think that sends the wrong message. Without substantive conversations about real classroom practice, not much transfer, reflection, or application to teaching practice will occur.

Joyce and Showers (2002) provide data to help us understand that without ongoing coaching conversations, the knowledge may increase, but the skills and transfer to the classroom will be relatively low. With ongoing coaching conversation, Joyce and Showers show that more than 90 percent of the knowledge and skills will be transferred to the classroom. We want teachers to use increased knowledge and skills to help teach students. Teachers want their students to learn well. Students deserve it.

Trust

We briefly mentioned trust before. Trust is the social lubricant that makes organizations run. When trust exists, organizations tend to think more creatively, take more risks, and share information more readily. There is a feeling of being supported. Wheatley and Kellner-Rogers (1996) declare that trust is the building block of an organization. Bryk and Schneider (2002) report about how important relational trust is for schools. They studied more than 250 elementary schools in Chicago public schools after the district implemented a site-based management model in some schools. They looked at five variables: school governance, curriculum, teaching techniques, professional development, and trust. What they found was that if you corrected for school governance, curriculum, teaching techniques, or professional development, the result was a 1 in 7 chance of positively affecting student achievement—not significant.

When they corrected for trust, they found a 1 in 2 chance of positively affecting student achievement. They looked at three different relationships regarding trust. Trust between administrators and teachers, between teachers and teachers, and parents and teachers.

All were significant. The most significant was between teachers and teachers.

Think about it, when teachers trust other teachers, they share more, help each other out, create more possibilities, and are supportive. We believe that is one of the outcomes important in schools and that PLCs promote and enhance those relationships.

Research by Bryk and Schneider (2002) and Tschannen-Moran (2004) maintain that trust among adults who are working in schools is a critical element necessary to increase student achievement. Tcshannen-Moran (2004) writes:

> Without trust, schools are likely to flounder in their attempts to provide constructive educational environments and meet the lofty goals that our society has set for them because energy needed to solve the complex problem of educating a diverse group of students is diverted into self-protection. (p. 15)

With trust, collegial learning and building communities will happen. Without trust, professionals tend to isolate and go their own way.

Reflective practice can help to close the knowing-doing gap. The collective knowledge and wisdom in our schools is our most valuable asset. As we embed reflective practice into the culture of the school through professional learning communities, we facilitate the transfer of information, we widen the use of effective practices, and trust is built through enhanced relationships. Sharing our human resources moves the organization ahead.

Conflict Management and Effectiveness

Based on conversations with educators, there continues to be massive overload for the adults working in educational systems. The demands continue to rise from inside and outside the organization. It seems that almost every solution to social issues becomes the responsibility of the school system. As mandates (funded and unfunded), legislative decisions, parent requests, and the pressure from community for improvement and accountability escalate, resources are being stretched beyond the limits. The rubber band is breaking, and the organization seems to be an unraveling. Under stress, people can turn on their organization and each other. The result is increasing conflict, especially among the adults.

Reasons for Conflict

Chadwick (1995) identifies five main reasons for conflict. They are change, power, scarcity, diversity, and civility. We have found that to be true in schools as well as the community. Change is the normal state and will continue into the future. Schools undertake change too many times, too quickly, and sometimes for political, not educational, reasons.

When there are power differentials, conflict happens. Those who see themselves without power will push for more attention and more input. Think of your school and your faculty. Has there been a time when a new curriculum or idea has been introduced? Did the faculty say, "Wow, we have been waiting for this" or did they say, "I am doing just fine, thank you very much"? Was the issue readily accepted or did it cause conflict within the system? The issue gets wrapped in a power struggle of who will make the decision and who will implement the changes. Power struggles can stop initiatives or reduce effectiveness.

Schools are in a scarcity situation. Think of all resources as either abundant or scarce. Yes, money and staffing seem always to be an issue. We don't think there will ever be enough money or staff. How about time as a resource? Time, as has been said earlier, will be a main issue as a resource. If time is scarce, what we do with the time we have signals importance. We think time is the most valuable nonrenewable resource we have. Where we spend our time signals importance. Will we have the courage to dedicate time for professional learning communities?

Diversity can cause conflict because of lack of understanding among cultures. An example occurred in a school district where we had a major influx of immigrants. A custom with this culture was washing their feet. Some students washed their feet in the drinking fountain. As you can imagine, the conflict between the students was enormous. The staff stepped forward to educate both the established culture and the immigrant culture, which resolved the problem. Wilson (1999) proclaimed, "Diversity strengthens." Diversity can strengthen cultures, or it can split them into factions. If we cannot address cognitive differences, how will we ever address issues around gender, ethnicity, race, or disabilities?

Finally, are we civil to each other? In working groups, we recommend norms be established and honored. Many times we work on short-term or long-term projects without ever talking about how we will work together. If meetings are not managed properly, the one who takes the most airtime or is the most assertive makes decisions. Meetings can be a great way to model how to deal effectively with diversity. How we treat individuals and groups with respect and dignity can be a great model for staff members. This can lead to increased participation and results in more trust.

Some resources for developing norms are Doyle and Straus (1976), Garmston and Wellman (1999), and Straus (2002). Whatever norms you agree to, it is important to make sure the behaviors match the norms. Some sample norms are putting ideas on the table, staying relevant to the issue being discussed, presuming positive intentions, actively listening, and so on.

A Conflict Management Strategy

We learned the following strategy from Chadwick (1995), and it can be used to manage conflict in the five areas noted. We focus on change; however, the same process can be and has been used in the other four categories. The important thing is to get all stakeholders in the same room. Leaving an ardent supporter of an issue outside the system will result in the issue's resurfacing.

To begin, arrange people in a circle so they can see each other. If there are more than eight or nine people, we recommend splitting into two groups. The goal is to make sure everyone has a chance to speak. The following questions are to be discussed, one at a time:

1. What are the issues surrounding this issue and how do you feel about it?

2. What is the worst possible outcome if we don't address this problem of change? What is the worst possible outcome if we do address this problem of change?

3. What is the best possible outcome if we don't address this problem of change? What is the best possible outcome if we do address this problem of change?

4. What beliefs and values are necessary for us to foster the best possible outcome?

5. What strategies and actions are you willing to take in order to foster the best possible outcomes?

6. What will be evidence that we are fostering our best possible outcome?

Choose a facilitator. The facilitator's job is to make sure everyone has a chance to speak and answer the first question. When everyone has had a chance to speak, the facilitator chooses a different facilitator. It is important to share the responsibility in the group. The new facilitator asks the second question.

We recommend chart paper and easels at this point. The current facilitator chooses another facilitator and then she or he becomes the recorder. The recorder writes down every word, not editing or modifying people's words. This builds trust. Words are sacred.

The current facilitator chooses a new facilitator and moves to the next question. And so on. At the end of the process, each group has generated answers to questions. The groups can either look for commonalities in order to build goals (fourth question), action plans (fifth question), or an assessment plan (sixth question).

The ultimate goal, then, is for the leadership and the group members to hold each other accountable for the goals, actions, and evidence they developed in a collective manner. Continuing to follow up and monitor the alignment of what are we doing with what we said we are going to do takes persistence, commitment, and reflection. Sometimes the discrepancy can cause conflict. Confronting issues forthrightly saves time and builds trust.

Leadership Implications

Leadership matters in organizations. The job of leaders is changing as everyone's job in education is changing. Zander and Zander (2000) offer some tips. One of the new leadership roles will be to engage and attract staff to a clear vision. Likewise, in the 12-step program of Alcoholics Anonymous, the eleventh tradition advocates for a program of attraction, not promotion. Many businesses promote sales through slick presentations, liberal interpretations of results, and incentives. Promoting sales is expensive for education. These techniques have varying success. On the other hand, if something is working in a school or a district, other schools and districts are attracted to them to find out what they are doing to get the successful results. Attracting is not the same as selling or promising perfection. Most of us in education have been sold snake oil for some problem. A leader must attract others to the vision, not sell them on it.

Zander and Zander (2000) also note that leaders must stop the downward spiral of conversations. This is another way leaders can make professional learning communities work—to speak in possibilities, not the downward spiral that sinks ideas. This is another way of saying clearly state what you want, not what you don't want. Create powerful teams by supporting people to be powerful. Being powerful is making it possible for people to do their best, contribute to others' learning, and take responsible risks for making learning happen.

Farson and Keyes's (2002) premise is if you are not making mistakes, you may not be learning as much as you could be. How do we treat others who make mistakes? Do we shoot them figuratively? Do we do eye rolls of disapproval? *Or* do we say, "What did we learn from that?" Here are two questions we can ask our colleagues and ourselves:

1. What have you contributed to someone over the past week?

2. What have you done that helped another person become better?

Leaders must help create space for conversations to take place during the school day. We know that ongoing, job-embedded, and results-driven professional learning increases application of new ideas and practices with staff. Providing time to talk and reflect about our teaching profession is a critical link to sustaining ongoing learning in the organization. In one school the principal assessed, "Unless we can find ways to reflect on our practice, we will not substantially change the way we do things. We will show up, give it our best shot, but will not be as effective as we could be."

Meetings can help create energy and possibilities through the connections that are made. Communicating ideas that generate new connections and lead to new actions can be extremely beneficial to the staff, the students, and the school. There are many resources for making meetings work. Doyle and Straus (1976), Harvey and Drolet (2004), and Garmston and Wellman (1999) are three resources for you. Meeting structures and how meetings operate are important, but how decision making is done can produce trust and collaboration that builds healthy organizations.

Vignette

An Urban School Reflects

An urban school decided to start a learning community. They had a couple of false starts the previous two years and then a new principal came.

A core group of 10 staff met with the principal to discuss how to involve more staff in leadership roles and to increase staff learning. After a couple more meetings, the goal of reflective practice was chosen as the main focus. A planning team was formed, and within one month the following structure was created.

Those who volunteered made a commitment to meet once a month for two hours. This meeting was divided into two parts: one hour on a new learning topic and one hour to reflect on applications to the school, the classroom, and personal uses.

Another commitment was for each person to meet in dyads or triads for one hour per week for reflective conferences on what they were individually learning and the effect the reflective practice program was having on their role in school leadership. Additionally, each participant was encouraged to journal on a daily basis. Professional development funds were used to promote these activities and to provide refreshments.

The result was 30 percent of the faculty met in the reflective practice process during the first year, there was 90 percent attendance at the reflection meetings, and 50 percent of the staff kept daily journals. The second year the participation rate increased to 45 percent attendance at the monthly meetings, and several school leadership teams formed to decide room assignments, campus goals, and professional development aligned with the School Improvement Plan. By the third year, 15 staff were trained to be facilitators in department meetings. For example, a physical education teacher was the facilitator for the world language department. This reduced the pressure of the world language teacher facilitating and being a member of the department at the same time. It is difficult to facilitate a meeting where your own budget, teaching assignments, and staffing issues are being discussed. Having outside department facilitators reduced conflict, communications and trust were increased, and school leadership expanded.

Rocks in the Road

Three concepts are noted here for your consideration: tension, intention, and attention.

Tension

Some tension is good. Complacency can kill organizations. Well-placed questions about what people want to happen compared to what is currently happening will sometimes generate dialogue. Keep stretching the goals and the thinking of staff. We suggest being relentless about asking questions related to what we are learning and what we want to know that works.

Intention

We all have good intentions. We want the best for our colleagues, our students, and ourselves. Good intention is not enough, however; we must articulate goals that represent our intentions. This means we have to identify *time* to meet, to set goals, and assume that adults want to learn to do things better, and that colleagues intend to share their expertise with others. Without these activities, it will be hard to establish or sustain professional learning communities.

Attention

Keep professional learning communities as the focus. Keep the light on. We suggest making things visual to focus attention on collegial learning. Keep the attention on learning by writing about it. Keep the attention on learning by experiencing learning in meetings, committee work, and faculty groups.

Engage in Learning Activities

1. As a principal, your language affects others. For one week, ask questions rather than make judgments. If you make statements, make sure there is no blame or judgment embedded in the comments.

    - What do you notice about the interactions with staff?
    - Were the conversations more creative, with richer dialogue?
    - What was the evidence that the conversations changed?

2. When facilitating meetings, start noticing the results of the following:

    - Is everyone getting a chance to speak?
    - Is trust being built so that authentic issues are being expressed in the meeting?
    - Are participants able to advocate for a position without degrading other ideas?

When we get home from a trip, we determine whether or not the trip was worth it in terms of fun, time, and money. Were my companions fun to be with? Did I spend too much or the right amount of money? Was the time away from home and work worth it?

We also evaluate the trip in emotional terms. Were the people we met along the way nice or unhelpful? Did it feel right being in the new environment? Did it feel good, bad, or indifferent? What would have made it better? What would we do next time?

There is also an assessment of what we did. Did we go to all the places we wanted to? Did we do all the things we wanted to? Did we bring the right equipment, clothes, and necessities? What would we do differently next time?

6

Where Are We?
Where Should We Be?
Who Is Monitoring
Our Work?

I'm still not comfortable using our student-focused constructivist learning approach in my classroom. . . . I wonder if I could bring this up in our PLC meeting and get some feedback.

Second grade teacher

We have rigorously assessed our students' progress on the new health program that we adopted last year in PLC. The kids are really into it and learning.

Tenth grade teacher

Harvey, how do you find out if your school's PLC is operating as well as it could be? Is there some way to know this?

One principal to another

Developing a culture of continuous assessment is an important component of a culture of continuous improvement. As we've noted, the professional learning community (PLC) is a significant vehicle for driving toward continuous improvement, but all too frequently checking progress, assessing, monitoring—whatever label you call it—is not used to make thoughtful decisions about supporting a professional learning community to reach high-quality implementation in a school.

Introducing a PLC into a school means introducing an innovation, for many of the school's professionals will never have experienced this way of learning together and working collegially together in a school. Eventually, this way of working becomes part of the culture of the school. But, in Chapter 1, we noted the implementation strategies that school leaders must supply if new programs, processes, or practices are to be taken on board and used well. One of these strategies is assessing or checking progress. The adoption and implementation of a PLC will not happen in one week, one month, or even one year. Therefore, the process of helping individuals learn how to act in a PLC and develop the skills needed (see Chapter 5) requires the monitoring of new behaviors as they are developing. Because there will be bumps, dips, and detours in the road to a well-performing PLC, someone must monitor the pulse of the individuals in the school to help ease them over the rough spots.

It is clear that what is assessed or monitored and given attention by the principal and other leaders (including teacher leaders) will be given attention by the remainder of the organization. Attending to how well each individual is operating in the PLC and understanding how and why each person is working enables the school leadership to provide assistance to all individuals. Assistance is the essential follow-up to assessment—the two go hand in hand. There is hardly any reason to assess or to check progress of how the PLC is becoming real to each professional in the school if support and follow-up are not provided to each person, based on the assessment.

When the PLC's principal routinely and regularly checks on implementation and gives support where it is needed, then high-quality development of the PLC flourishes. It should be noted here that the principal engages in this activity, but also engages others. This task is time demanding and should be shared. Ultimately, when the PLC is well developed, then the participants will be doing the monitoring, or assessing and assisting, of each other.

It is vital that the informal and the occasional formal data that result from assessing progress are studied, analyzed, carefully interpreted, and used to guide the interventions (help and assistance) given to each individual.

We propose that the following three levels of assessment be employed in a school that is operating or developing as a community of professional learners:

1. Assessment to understand how well the PLC is functioning

2. Assessment to ascertain how well PLC members are transferring their learning in their PLC (about curriculum, instruction, assessment, and so on) into their work environment (teachers' classrooms, principals' settings)

3. Assessment to identify impact on student gains that accrue as a result of the staff's PLC work

The ultimate purpose of the professional learning community is the attainment of identified student results. Linking the collegial learning of the PLC members with their resultant school and classroom practice to student outcomes is essential. Thus, these levels provide three questions around which we structure this chapter:

1. How or by what means can the operation of a professional learning community be assessed?

2. How can PLC members be monitored to learn how they are transferring their community learning into their work settings?

3. How can student gains be assessed and linked to the work of the professional learning community?

In this chapter we explore ways to monitor or check progress of the staff as a PLC, examine how well the staff is implementing what they have learned with their PLC colleagues, and determine what results are being realized for students.

Assessing the Professional Learning Community Operation

How well the PLC is functioning in a school should be a persistent question and one that is given careful scrutiny. Monitoring can be done formally (thus, probably infrequently) and informally (which should be done continually).

Formal Assessment

An instrument exists that can be used to explore the degree to which a school is performing as a PLC. The School Professional Staff as Learning Community instrument (Hord, 2000a) is framed around the five research-based attributes of a PLC reported in Chapter 1. While it is a short, 17-item instrument, it has been rigorously tested for validity and reliability (Meehan, Orletsky, & Sattes, 1997) and can provide a helicopter view of the school's work as a PLC. It has been used extensively in implementation studies (some of which have been dissertation studies) to ascertain the progress being made in a school's efforts to become a professional learning community. Participants mark this rubriclike instrument, then each of the items can be scored as means. A profile can be created to indicate where the staff is strong on the attributes and where more attention is needed.

Alternatively, this instrument has been employed as a protocol for interviewing respondents in a qualitative manner, observing the conventions of qualitative research. These results give illumination about how the individuals in the school perceive the PLC and can provide information about its operation. Aggregating the responses for a group picture may be done, or using the responses for each individual is especially powerful. In either case, the purpose to be served is to use a process of rigor—not just one's opinions—to judge progress of the professionals in reaching their goal of operating as a learning community and providing assistance where each needs it.

Informal Procedures

In Chapter 5 we mentioned using the walk-through as part of establishing a reflective practice. Walk-throughs provide an informal means for collecting information about how the PLC is operating in the school. The walk-through is mostly what the label says: one walks about to various grade level or department professional learning team meetings, and to the whole faculty community as it meets, to observe PLC activity. It can also be used to observe a teacher who has been invited to visit another for a particular purpose (peers helping peers, an example of the fifth PLC attribute, shared personal practice). A form, or protocol, is advised in order to maintain focus on the elements of the PLC under examination. Typically this visit by the principal or other PLC leader is brief, 10–15 minutes in the meeting space, without interruption of the individuals or group. It is followed by feedback to those observed, with ideas solicited for acting on the feedback.

Hall and Hord (2006) recommend the one-legged interview or informal conference to learn how things are going with the implementation of new practice and to understand the concerns that the implementers have about the new program, practice, or process (see Chapter 2 for more on the one-legged interview). The professional learning community is a new way of working, thus a new practice. The informal interview or conference can be used to learn how things are going with the community processes in its small teams and with the whole faculty. Questions to be asked about the PLC operations and strategies should be few in number and clear to the inquirer. Having these one-to-one or small group conversations indicates to the participants that their efforts are valuable and worthy of attention, support, and assistance.

Observing the whole faculty professional learning community's behaviors and deliberations is an important opportunity for identifying how well the community of professional learners is working together democratically and collegially. Again, a structure, either on paper or mentally, that guides the observation is helpful in gaining the impressions and information that are desired. Making notes is a good idea so that the information gleaned is accurate.

Do you share the formally or informally derived information with the community? Yes, the PLC is a collaborative endeavor, and being open and transparent, as mentioned earlier in this book, is important. Sharing information about individuals, of course, is not appropriate, but reporting the generalizations derived from aggregating information across the community allows the members to know how they are progressing—where they are strong in their attributes of a PLC and where additional attention should be given. The group should be solicited for ideas and input regarding how to address the areas that need attention. Also, they should be given the opportunity to volunteer to take action based upon that input.

Monitoring Members' Transfer of Their PLC Learning

We cannot emphasize enough that the major purpose of the PLC is the *learning* in which the adults in the school engage. When the professionals learn new practices, different instructional strategies, and exciting curriculum, they become more effective with their students—and, then, students learn more successfully. Thus, an important aspect of the PLC is not only how well the PLC is functioning as an infrastructure or way of working, but how well the staff put into practice what they decided to learn, in order to serve students more effectively. It is easy to see that if the staff left their learning in the community meeting and never implemented it into their classroom practice, the purpose of the PLC would not be realized. The question becomes, "How do we assess or monitor the staff's implementation of new practice?"

Change process research has produced tools for assessing the degree of implementation evolving in the teacher's classroom or in the principal's office. The three diagnostic tools noted in this chapter are part of the Concern-Based Adoption Model (CBAM): the Stages of Concern, the Levels of Use, and Innovation Configurations (Hall & Hord, 2006).

Stages of Concern

Researchers at the Research and Development Center for Teacher Education at the University of Texas identified seven Stages of Concern (SoC) among educators who were adopting an innovation—whether it was a product, curriculum, set of strategies, or an entire program that contained multiple innovations (George, Hall, & Stiegelbauer, 2006). The concerns of implementers, or those at the brink of implementing new practices that they have been learning in professional development sessions, from mentors or from their colleagues in the community of professional learners, can be identified in several ways. The broadest assessment reveals whether the individual has "self" concerns, "task" concerns, or "impact" concerns (see Figure 6.1). Recognizing and understanding individuals' concerns can serve as a gauge that informs their need for assistance in implementing new practices. Again, the formula for monitoring new practices is to assess and assist. Individuals' concerns can be revealed using three different approaches that range in formality and time required.

Stages of Concern Questionnaire

This 35-item survey has a long history of use and has been utilized in studies around the globe, as it has been translated into multiple languages. The individual quickly marks the 35 statements using a scale of 0 to 6 to indicate how true the statement is to the individual at the time. The scores are changed into percentiles, and a profile of the individual's concerns is produced, indicating self, task, impact concerns, and with more specificity, where the respondent is on the seven stages. Please refer to the Stages of Concern technical manual for more information (George, Hall, & Stiegelbauer, 2006).

Figure 6.1   The Stages of Concern About an Innovation

IMPACT	6	Refocusing	The individual focuses on exploring ways to reap more universal benefits from the innovation, including the possibility of making major changes to it or replacing it with a more powerful alternative.
	5	Collaboration	The individual focuses on coordinating and cooperating with others regarding use of the innovation.
	4	Consequence	The individual focuses on the innovation's impact on students in his or her immediate sphere of influence. Considerations include the relevance of the innovation for students; the evaluation of student outcomes, including performance and competencies; and the changes needed to improve student outcomes.
TASK	3	Management	The individual focuses on the processes and tasks of using the innovation and the best use of information and resources. Issues related to efficiency, organizing, managing, and scheduling dominate.
SELF	2	Personal	The individual is uncertain about the demands of the innovation, his or her adequacy to meet those demands, and/or his or her role with the innovation. The individual is analyzing his or her relationship to the reward structure of the organization, determining his or her part in decision making, and considering potential conflicts with existing structures or personal commitment. Concerns also might involve the financial or status implications of the program for the individual and his or her colleagues.
	1	Informational	The individual indicates a general awareness of the innovation and interest in learning more details about it. The individual does not seem to be worried about himself or herself in relation to the innovation. Any interest is in impersonal, substantive aspects of the innovation, such as its general characteristics, effects, and requirements for use.
	0	Unconcerned	The individual indicates little concern about or involvement with the innovation.

SOURCE: From *Measuring Implementation in Schools: The Stages of Concern Questionnaire* by Archie A. George, Gene E. Hall, and Suzanne M. Stiegelbauer. Reprinted with permission from the Southwest Educational Development Laboratory, Austin, TX.

The Stages of Concern Questionnaire (SoCQ) is the most formal way of identifying concerns individuals may have and is the most rigorous means. Respondents require 15–20 minutes to mark the survey, and it is easily scored either by hand or by computer program. The scores can be produced as profiles for individuals, or with computer aggregation profiles can be generated for small (grade-level or department teachers) and large groups (whole faculty). Although it does not require much time for its administration and processing and it provides results in which one can place great confidence, some don't like its formality.

Open-Ended Statements

A more informal way of learning individuals' concerns is administered by giving implementers a blank piece of paper that has written at the top the following direction:

When you think about [the new practice that you have been learning and are implementing] what concerns do you have? Please be frank, and answer in complete sentences.

The responses are then content analyzed, which requires more time than processing the SoCQ, but gives indicators of the individual's concerns and also typically provides information about why they have the concerns that they have expressed. This information gives the principal or other leaders more understanding about the individuals and how to help them implement new ways of working.

Informal Interviews

The "one-legged interview" was noted earlier in this chapter. This procedure is by far the most informal in its data collection process, and frequently the person being queried about their concerns does not realize it. Conducting this conversation with a person speaks to the individual, causing the person to feel valued for their opinions and worthy of engaging in the work being done.

Before using the open-ended statement, the informal interview, or the 35-item questionnaire, training is highly recommended, as is studying the technical manual (George, Hall & Stiegelbauer, 2006) or other materials (Hall & Hord, 2006; Hord, Rutherford, Huling-Austin, & Hall, 2004).

One can also use the idea of Stages of Concern in a *really* informal way. That is, by keeping the framework of the seven Stages of Concern in mind (sort of as a "hearing" aid) while listening to conversations and interactions in the teachers' workroom, lounge, or other gathering places. Ultimately, it would be quite helpful for the community of professionals to learn a bit about Stages of Concern in order to help them to understand their own change process or implementation development, and as a way to understand colleagues and offer assistance.

Levels of Use

A second implementation tool is the Levels of Use (LoU) concept and its measures. The LoU includes eight levels, or groupings, of how individuals act or behave when learning and implementing new practice. LoU has been verified through research (Hall, Dirksen, & George, 2006). Each of the levels is operationally described as a person moves from nonuse of new practices to renewal, making modifications to the original practice to benefit clients (that is, students are the principals' and teachers' clients). An interview, of which there are two kinds, is the means by which to assess a person's level of use.

LoU Branching Interview

As in the one-legged interview, the respondent is visited in a brief and casual way to gain a broad view of the person's Level of Use. When we know whether the person is at level 0, doing nothing relative to implementing new practice, or whether the person is at preparation, getting ready to start doing the practice, or has been engaged long term and is considering refinement, then we can judge the state of implementation. Having done this assessment, appropriate assistance can be given. Conducting a LoU branching interview requires training and development of the skills and should not be attempted without it (Hall & Hord, 2006).

LoU Focused Interview

A more formal interview, also requiring considerable training of persons planning to use it, is the focused interview. One uses a protocol and collects abundant information in order to identify where the person falls on the Levels of Use continuum and where the person can be described via eight levels of use. This procedure is more rigorous and digs into deeper detail. This interview is not often used to facilitate implementation, but for research and evaluation purposes.

Because observable behaviors are the focus of attention, many people prefer this measure to the Stages of Concern, which reveals the more affective side of implementation. It is conceivable that the community of professional learners could be enabled to understand and to use Levels of Use in a very informal way, allowing them to provide appropriate assistance to their colleagues.

Innovation Configurations

A third concept and measure from the CBAM is that of Innovation Configurations (IC). Whereas the SoC and LoU assess the *individual* and their progress on implementation, the IC defines *what* constitutes the practice, program, or process that is being implemented.

Experienced change researchers and practitioners lament the lack of understanding that individuals typically have about new programs or practices that they are learning about and trying to implement. The IC provides the description of the new practice, the precision needed so that all implementers can agree on the goal toward which they are collectively working. The IC also recognizes that implementing new practice, even when the implementers have collegially decided to take it on board, requires a great deal of time, support, and assistance, and that it is a developmental process. Thus, high-quality implementation is a goal toward which all are working but acknowledge that full implementation will take time.

The IC Map is a rubriclike instrument that defines the major components of the new program or practice and describes the components in their most desirable state. A continuum for each component suggests how the components will look over time as individuals learn to do the new work. An example of such a map comes from a publication that describes the National Staff Development Council (NSDC) staff development standards (Roy & Hord, 2003). Maps were created for the 12 standards for five role groups: teachers, principals, central office staff, superintendents, and school board. The maps in Figures 6.2 and 6.3 exemplify one of the components of the first NSDC standard related to learning communities, and the subjects of the maps are the principal and teachers. These maps illustrate how the principal's and teachers' work are related.

Such maps are created at the time that the professional learning community has elected to take on a new practice. They provide mental pictures of the new practice in action and are used as a tool to communicate to all what the practice is and the expectations for individuals' involvement.

Figure 6.2 Principal's Role in Creating and Supporting Learning Communities

Staff development that has as its goal high levels of learning for all students, teachers, and administrators requires a form of professional learning that is quite different from the workshop-driven approach. The most powerful forms of staff development occur in ongoing teams that meet on a regular basis, preferably several times a week, for the purposes of learning, joint lesson planning, and problem solving. These teams, often called learning communities or communities of practice, operate with a commitment to the norms of continuous improvement and experimentation and engage their members in improving their daily work to advance the achievement of school district and school goals for student learning.

Learning teams may be of various sizes and serve different purposes. For instance, the faculty as a whole may meet once or twice a month to reflect on its work, engage in appropriate learning, and assess its progress. In addition, some members of the faculty may serve on school improvement teams or committees that focus on the goals and methods of schoolwide improvement. While these teams make important contributions to school culture,

learning environment and other priority issues, they do not substitute for the day-to-day professional conversations focused on instructional issues that are the hallmark of effective learning communities.

Learning teams meet almost every day and concern themselves with practical ways to improve teaching and learning. Members of learning communities take collective responsibility for the learning of all students represented by team members. Teacher members of learning teams, which consist of four to eight members, assist one another in examining the standards students are required to master, planning more effective lessons, critiquing student work, and solving the common problems of teaching.

The teams determine the areas in which additional learning would be helpful and read articles, attend workshops or courses, or invite consultants to assist them in acquiring necessary knowledge or skills. In addition to the regular meetings, participants observe one another in the classroom and conduct other job-related responsibilities. Learning communities are strengthened when other support staff, administrators, and even school board members choose to participate, and

when communication is facilitated between teams. Because of this common focus and clear direction, problems of fragmentation and incoherence that typically thwart school improvement efforts are eliminated.

Administrator learning communities also meet on a regular basis to deepen participants' understanding of instructional leadership, identify practical ways to assist teachers in improving the quality of student work, critique one another's school improvement efforts, and learn important skills such as data analysis and providing helpful feedback to teachers.

Many educators also benefit from participation in regional or national subject-matter networks or school reform consortia that connect schools with common interests. While most such networks have face-to-face meetings, increasing numbers of participants use electronic means such as e-mail, listservs, and bulletin boards to communicate between meetings or as a substitute for meetings. Such virtual networks can provide important sources of information and knowledge as well as the interpersonal support required to persist over time in changing complex schoolwide or classroom practices.

(Continued)

123

Figure 6.2 (Continued)

The Principal

Content
Process
Context

DESIRED OUTCOME 1.1: Prepares teachers for skillful collaboration.

LEVEL 1	LEVEL 2	LEVEL 3	LEVEL 4	LEVEL 5	LEVEL 6
Ensures that the role of group facilitator becomes the responsibility of everyone and rotates as the skill level of group members increases. Provides training and support to develop faculty members to serve as skilled facilitators who provide support during whole school and learning team meetings.	Provides training and support to develop faculty members to serve as skilled facilitators who provide support during whole school and learning team meetings.	Provides opportunities for team leaders to learn about group process, group dynamics, the stages of group development, and group decision making. Schedules multiple sessions throughout the year as well as coaching experiences.	Provides support to learning teams and/or whole school meetings throughout the stages of group development by supplying a skilled group facilitator.	Does not provide teachers professional development to build collaboration skills.	

DESIRED OUTCOME 1.2: Creates an organizational structure that supports collegial learning.

LEVEL 1	LEVEL 2	LEVEL 3	LEVEL 4	LEVEL 5	LEVEL 6
Persists with a regular schedule for collegial interaction in the face of resistance. Structures time for teacher reflection about their learning. Monitors to ensure the time is used well.	Structures the daily and/or weekly schedule for regular meeting times during the school day for collegial interaction. Monitors to ensure the time is used well.	Uses staff meetings for collegial interaction and sharing. Grade-level and content area groups meet throughout the year with the goal of sharing ideas, resources, and curricula.	Does not adapt the structure of the school to accommodate collegial learning.		

DESIRED OUTCOME 1.3: Understands and implements an incentive system that ensures collaborative work.

LEVEL 1	LEVEL 2	LEVEL 3	LEVEL 4	LEVEL 5	LEVEL 6
Works with teachers to create and implement an incentive system for learning teams. Recognizes and rewards joint work that results in student gains and accomplishes school goals.	Recognizes and rewards teams for working together to accomplish school goals and increase student learning.	Creates structures and processes to ensure there is mutual support among teachers while expecting each person to focus work on school goals and outcomes.	Requests that faculty members cooperate with each other.	Does not implement a support system for collaborative work.	

(Continued)

125

Figure 6.2 (Continued)

DESIRED OUTCOME 1.4: Creates and maintains a learning community to support teacher and student learning.

LEVEL 1	LEVEL 2	LEVEL 3	LEVEL 4	LEVEL 5	LEVEL 6
Builds a culture that respects risk taking, encourages collegial exchange, identifies and resolves conflict, sustains trust, and engages the whole staff as a learning community to improve the learning of all students.	Works with faculty to create a variety of learning teams to attain different goals. Facilitates conflict resolution among group members. Supports learning teams by providing articles, videos, and other activities for use during team time.	Works with faculty to create learning teams with clear goals, outcomes, and results outlined in writing. Expects and reviews team logs each month in order to coordinate activities within and among the teams.	Creates ad hoc study teams without clear direction or accountability.	Does not create learning teams.	

DESIRED OUTCOME 1.5: Participates with other administrators in one or more learning communities.

LEVEL 1	LEVEL 2	LEVEL 3	LEVEL 4	LEVEL 5	LEVEL 6
Attends regularly learning community meetings organized at the district, regional, state, and/or national level to identify and solve school challenges, as well as to learn together.	Meets regularly with a district learning team to solve school challenges and learn together.	Meets informally with administrative colleagues to discuss school challenges.	Provides support to learning teams and/or whole school meetings throughout the stages of group development by supplying a skilled group facilitator.	Does not participate in any learning community.	

SOURCE: Reprinted from *Moving NSDC's Staff Development Standards Into Practice: Innovation Configurations*, by Pat Roy and Shirley Hord (NSDC, 2003) with permission of the National Staff Development Council, www.nsdc.org, 2006. All rights reserved.

Figure 6.3   Teachers' Role in Participating in Learning Communities

Staff development that has as its goal high levels of learning for all students, teachers, and administrators requires a form of professional learning that is quite different from the workshop-driven approach. The most powerful forms of staff development occur in ongoing teams that meet on a regular basis, preferably several times a week, for the purposes of learning, joint lesson planning, and problem solving. These teams, often called learning communities or communities of practice, operate with a commitment to the norms of continuous improvement and experimentation and engage their members in improving their daily work to advance the achievement of school district and school goals for student learning.

Learning teams may be of various sizes and serve different purposes. For instance, the faculty as a whole may meet once or twice a month to reflect on its work, engage in appropriate learning, and assess its progress. In addition, some members of the faculty may serve on school improvement teams or committees that focus on the goals and methods of schoolwide improvement. While these teams make important contributions to school culture, learning environment and other priority issues, they do not substitute for the day-to-day professional conversations focused on instructional issues that are the hallmark of effective learning communities.

Learning teams meet almost every day and concern themselves with practical ways to improve teaching and learning. Members of learning communities take collective responsibility for the learning of all students represented by team members. Teacher members of learning teams, which consist of four to eight members, assist one another in examining the standards students are required to master, planning more effective lessons, critiquing student work, and solving the common problems of teaching.

The teams determine areas in which additional learning would be helpful and read articles, attend workshops or courses, or invite consultants to assist them in acquiring necessary knowledge or skills. In addition to the regular meetings, participants observe one another in the classroom and conduct other job-related responsibilities. Learning communities are strengthened when other support staff, administrators, and even school board members choose to participate, and when communication is facilitated between teams. Because of this common focus and clear direction, problems of fragmentation and incoherence that typically thwart school improvement efforts are eliminated.

Administrator learning communities also meet on a regular basis to deepen participants' understanding of instructional leadership, identify practical ways to assist teachers in improving the quality of student work, critique one another's school improvement efforts, and learn important skills such as data analysis and providing helpful feedback to teachers.

Many educators also benefit from participation in regional or national subject-matter networks or school reform consortia that connect schools with common interests. While most such networks have face-to-face meetings, increasing numbers of participants use electronic means such as e-mail, listservs, and bulletin boards to communicate between meetings or as a substitute for meetings. Such virtual networks can provide important sources of information and knowledge as well as the interpersonal support required to persist over time in changing complex schoolwide or classroom practices.

(Continued)

127

Figure 6.3 (Continued)

The Teacher

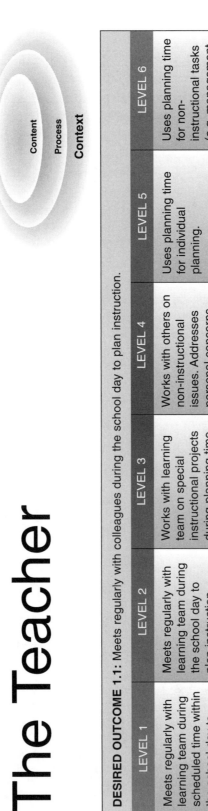

Content
Process
Context

DESIRED OUTCOME 1.1: Meets regularly with colleagues during the school day to plan instruction.

LEVEL 1	LEVEL 2	LEVEL 3	LEVEL 4	LEVEL 5	LEVEL 6
Meets regularly with learning team during scheduled time within the school day to develop lesson plans, examine student work, monitor student progress, assess the effectiveness of instruction, and identify needs for professional learning.	Meets regularly with learning team during the school day to plan instruction, examine student work, and monitor student progress.	Works with learning team on special instructional projects during planning time.	Works with others on non-instructional issues. Addresses personal concerns, not group issues.	Uses planning time for individual planning.	Uses planning time for non-instructional tasks (e.g. management, personal tasks).

DESIRED OUTCOME 1.2: Aligns collaborative work with school improvement goals.

LEVEL 1	LEVEL 2	LEVEL 3	LEVEL 4	LEVEL 5	LEVEL 6
Participates frequently with all professional staff members to discuss, document and demonstrate how their work aligns with school and district goals. Engages in professional learning with colleagues to support this work.	Aligns the work of the learning team with schoolwide goals. Works in a learning team (grade-level, subject matter, interdisciplinary, vertical) to address issues related to the grade or subject area.	Works in a learning team (grade-level, subject matter, interdisciplinary, vertical) to address issues related to specific grade or subject area.	Works alone; addresses individual issues rather than school or grade-level issues.		

DESIRED OUTCOME 1.3: Participates in learning teams, some of whose membership extends beyond the school.

LEVEL 1	LEVEL 2	LEVEL 3	LEVEL 4	LEVEL 5	LEVEL 6
Participates in state, regional, districtwide, and/or national networks. Participates in interdisciplinary or subject matter and grade-level learning teams.	Participates in districtwide and regional networks and interdisciplinary or subject matter and grade-level learning teams.	Participates in both interdisciplinary and subject matter and grade-level learning teams within the district.	Participates in interdisciplinary learning teams and/or subject matter or grade-level teams only.	Participates in individual learning outside grade-level, subject area, and/or school.	

SOURCE: Reprinted from *Moving NSDC's Staff Development Standards Into Practice: Innovation Configurations*, by Pat Roy and Shirley Hord (NSDC, 2003) with permission of the National Staff Development Council, www.nsdc.org, 2006. All rights reserved.

At any point in time, individuals may mark themselves on the map, or in consultation with colleagues, or with a consultant or facilitator of the work. The map can provide clear descriptions of where the individual needs to focus attention, learning, and implementation. Thus, the map is a very useful monitoring device, indicating where the person is and where to move next.

Because the individual, a group of individuals such as a grade-level team, or the entire faculty can use the map to reflect on their own progress and then target the help needed or the attention required, it may well be the most practical and useful of the three diagnostic tools discussed in this chapter. It sets the goals for action and the steps that may be involved in getting there. A principal, leadership team, or others may use the map to monitor progress and recommend support. In fact, any person in the community can use an IC Map to monitor individual progress and to work collegially in helping peers to assess their progress and to determine what needs to be done.

Again, training in creating a map for a particular practice and in how to use it provides everyone in the community with the knowledge and skills to self-assess and to help others in their assessment. See the manual for Innovation Configurations (Hord, Stiegelbauer, Hall, & George, 2006).

Linking Professional Learning to Student Results

We have been using a theory of professional development to illuminate the work of the professional learning community. Figure 1.3, which represents this theory, indicates how the design and delivery of professional learning develops and nurtures specified practices that principals and teachers can use to increase their effectiveness. The identified practices have been selected to address students' learning needs. At this point, we present a modified Figure 1.3 here, as Figure 6.4.

To the original Figure 1.3, we have added an Innovation Configuration Map to indicate what the principals and teachers will be doing to reach the desired student outcomes and how professional learning will inform the principals and teachers and enable them to develop these practices. The desired student outcomes have been identified by the professional learning community through examination and study of student data; the new principal and teacher knowledge and skills that relate to the students' needs have been specified by the professional learning community; and, professional learning

Figure 6.4   The Relationship Between Professional Learning Indicated by the IC Map and Student Learning

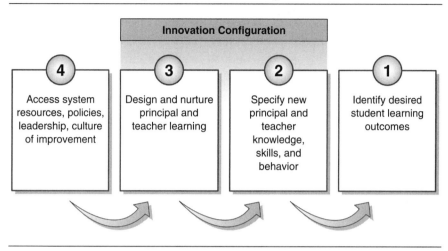

has been dictated and designed by the professional learning community to develop the knowledge and skills of the principals and teachers. The Innovation Configuration Map in Figure 6.4 is identical for Boxes 2 and 3, for the professional learning (3) must achieve the skills required by the staff (2) to produce the outcomes desired in students.

In this chapter we have suggested numerous ways to monitor the development and quality operation of the professional learning community—its strategies, structures, and practices—to continuously assess and provide support and assistance where it is needed by the community. We have provided numerous formal and informal means by which to check the progress of the PLC members in their implementation and use of their new learning in the school and their classrooms, learning derived from their PLC study and learning activities. However, the bottom line is whether the PLC has served students well, for this is the PLC's goal and purpose for existing.

We must be certain that the professional learning opportunities provided in Box 3 are aligned with what the PLC members need for acquiring the identified knowledge and skills in Box 2, which are aligned with the student results desired in Box 1. Monitoring the operation of the PLC is ongoing and supported, and focuses professional learning that nurtures staff's capacity to gain specified student outcomes. We have discussed how to monitor the staff's gains so that their learning and implementation are supported. Now, are students successfully learning what we have given focus?

Which Student Outcomes?

There are numerous outcomes that may be gained by the staff when it is working as a PLC. These have been cited from the research in Chapter 1 of this book. The focus now is on students. In examining student gains, the focus of inquiry is on those gains or lack of gains identified by the PLC as in need of attention, and for which staff have been acquiring new knowledge, skills, and behaviors. We are not looking at general overall student achievement, but at those specific competencies, skills, and so on that have been identified by the PLC as in need of improvement. It is nice to know that the school as a whole has moved from the lowest quartile (before the staff organized into a PLC) to the highest quartile of student achievement in the district on the state assessment test (after it became a performing PLC). The real question is, Has the staff learning in the PLC resulted in the student gains specified by the community of professionals?

Who Monitors Student Results?

Everyone! The principal, the faculty, the students themselves. This monitoring of student learning is ongoing and ever present, and develops a culture of continuous assessment leading to continuous improvement—provided, of course, that the assessment data are acted on and attention given to data-based decisions that lead to actions for improvement. This suggests that each student's progress is observed and monitored by classroom teachers. This progress is monitored also by the principal. And, even students in the elementary grades can be given charts of their learning objectives and taught to monitor their progress. To be in classrooms where students can report the goals and/or objectives of the activities in which they are involved, and how they will know when they have achieved those objectives well, is very exciting.

When to Monitor Student Results?

Constantly! To reiterate what has already been stated, student learning assessment is ongoing, ever present, and always under surveillance. The wise members of a PLC consistently take note through various means to determine how and if students are learning the specified knowledge, skills, behaviors, and developing desired attitudes, beliefs, and relationships. This is done daily, weekly, monthly, quarterly, semiannually, and at the end of the year. Student assessment does not wait until the annual state achievement test administration and reporting. Because this monitoring is done continuously, the staff should be able easily to predict how well students will score on the annual tests.

How to Monitor Student Outcomes?

We have been discussing monitoring in terms of (1) the operation of the PLC, (2) the PLC members' transfer of their community learning into classrooms, and, now, (3) student learning as a result of the professionals' learning. As in the previous two sections of this chapter, there are both formal and informal ways to monitor this student learning.

Formal Student Assessment

Many individuals, when asked how student outcomes should be measured and monitored, respond about their particular state's standardized achievement test. Most certainly this measure is currently an important one, for political and economic consequences can derive from its results. Many states have developed policies that have specific implications for schools and students, so realistically, much attention must be given to these tests.

Results from these tests provide rich data about how well students (and by inference the staff) are doing related to the content tested. Most certainly, these tests should be given attention for this reason. After all, aren't most of these tests grounded in the basic skills that most everyone expects students to be able to demonstrate? It is unfortunate that, in many cases, an exceedingly large amount of pressure and an exceptionally small amount of time for educators to enable students to do well on these tests have been provided. Nonetheless, state achievement tests, administered annually, provide data useful to the PLC for monitoring student progress.

Other formal assessments are standardized tests that some states may use in addition to the "state test," with these tests containing nationally recognized content and skills to be tested. While parts of these tests are useful to the PLC in learning how well students are mastering the particular learning elements addressed by the PLC, it means examining much data to find those data that are of particular relevance to the PLC's goals for students.

There may also be district-generated tests for use in particular districts for the various subjects that students are expected to master.

These assessments are typically coupled with a district curriculum guide so that student outcomes of interest in the curriculum guide may be tested. Again, these tests that "cover the waterfront" of all subjects and disciplines may not be tailored well for the PLC use. However, this array of formal assessments has utility for the PLC in that they can provide professionals with data about student gains in relationship to national norms. These monitoring "schema" may be thought of as summative, while the informal means are designed for formative use.

Informal Student Monitoring

Good teachers in classrooms monitor their students' work daily for its quality. One of Madeleine Hunter's admonitions that educators remember well today is her "monitor and adjust" instructional strategy (Hunter, 1976), based on students' accomplishments of learning objectives. This means that teachers have keen eyes and ears and attention to what and how students are doing their learning. These are the observations that teachers (and principals in their walk-throughs) make as they move about the classroom "eavesdropping" on students. These data are gathered informally, but the teacher has a clear picture in mind of the accomplishment of the learning task and how the student will accomplish it. Needless to say, what is of particular observation and attention are the specific learning goals identified by the PLC, and for which the staff have been engaged in their own learning to become more effective in producing these results in students. These data are used on the spot to correct students' work and their achievement. For the purpose of immediacy, this strategy of student monitoring is imperative.

Examining student work has been the subject of many schools' attention in the past several years. There are multiple protocols for doing this, but essentially, teachers bring examples of student work to a common meeting at which a critique or rubric is used to judge the quality of the work. A protocol is used to guide the work of the teachers in their examination. This could be an exceptionally promising activity for the PLC that had previously identified specific student products that exemplify the PLC's specific student learning goals. Obviously, such an assessment activity provides data that can be used for students' immediate relearning or celebration of work well done by the students. Again, the PLC is looking at student work to assess students' need for continuing assistance and to identify staff's needs for additional learning.

Just as the informal conference can be used with teachers and administrators to ascertain how well they are implementing their community learning, the informal conference may be used with students. Principals and teachers may have individual chats with students in order to gain insight into students' understanding of learning tasks, to find "glitches" in the instructional strategies, and to gain data for reteaching. The focus in this little conference is on how well the student is mastering the desired outcomes that the PLC has identified.

Noted earlier in this discussion of monitoring student progress is student self-monitoring. This is an important skill for students and gives them ready insights into their own learning and how well they are progressing. However, students must be given the means by which to do this, and learn how to assess themselves. As students become skilled at assessing themselves in an objective way, they can be instructed about how to assess each other. This should not be undertaken until the students understand fully why they are given the privilege of assessing themselves and others, and have developed the maturity, respect, and regard for each other so that they give and receive feedback appropriately. Clearly, these informal assessments or monitoring activities are for formative purposes, that is, judging where students are in their learning attainment and using the data to assist students to a higher level and quality of learning.

Leadership Implications

It is at the stage of monitoring the implementation of new practices, programs, or structures, such as the professional learning community, that the innovation can move toward success. Monitoring requires a sincere commitment from the leadership of the school or other organization. It is easy to assume that because individuals had the opportunity to learn new practices, and this is assuredly more powerful when the learning is done with others, that they now have the knowledge and skills, the expertise to put the new ideas into routine operation. We have learned over and over that this is fallacious.

Staff development research reports to us loud and clear that it is the follow-up (assessing and assisting), the checking back with individuals as they are trying to use new ideas in their work setting, that makes or breaks the success of implementation (Joyce & Showers, 2002). This strategy of checking progress, or monitoring, requires a great deal of patience and persistence from the leadership of the school.

Persistence

The monitoring tools introduced and described earlier in this chapter may be used to good advantage by the monitoring leader. The walk-through can be tailored for observing teachers as they work as a community and as they implement their community learning in their classrooms. The informal conference is a very useful tool for inquiring into a teacher's work to discover how things are going and to identify needs that have not been met. Both these strategies can be introduced and over time the staff will become comfortable with the activities. Persist in the action, even though there may be some staff who are not comfortable initially.

The persistent principal, in exercising these activities, demonstrates caring and concern for the changes in practice that the community has collectively decided upon. The walk-throughs and informal conferences should be open and transparent, with feedback given to the teacher in an appropriate way. The idea is to continually strengthen the community's new ways of working, and much focused attention must be given so that the PLC's precise goals are reached. Here again, as in Chapter 4, we think Collins's Hedgehog Concept is important to keep in mind. Collins (2005) explains that, "the essence of the Hedgehog Concept is to attain piercing clarity about how to produce the best long-term results, and then exercising the relentless discipline to say, 'No thank you' to opportunities that fail the hedgehog test" (p. 80).

Ultimately, as noted earlier, when the professional learning community has generated respectful attitudes across the community, has developed high regard among all members, and trust has been established, then the community members will take on the responsibility of checking progress for each other and supporting peers when their needs have been identified.

Patience

While persistence, based on commitment, is the operable word, leaders must also demonstrate patience. All individuals do not change or take on new practice at the same time or rate. Stages of Concern and Levels of Use help us to know the truth of this statement. And these tools can be used by the monitoring leader to understand staff concerns that may be interfering with their implementation. Taking time to understand the affect (SoC) that the new way of working has on individuals is useful in determining the best means for helping the individual to move forward. Considering LoU as a lens for observing the behaviors of teachers as a walk-through is conducted, provides focus to the observation. Again, some individuals need more time to master new programs and practices than others. Patience is necessary in order not to overwhelm people, but persistence is also necessary to keep everyone in the game.

Celebrations for small efforts or large are definitely in order. Commendations for individuals can be made publicly or privately. An ice cream sundae party for everyone is a supportive gesture and can sweeten the implementation. Notes that are personalized can be placed in teachers' mailboxes as a private way to acknowledge their efforts. These celebrations, even if quite small, are appreciated and will encourage everyone in their work toward reaching the student goals that have been articulated.

Vignette

Data . . . Macadamia Nut Cookies . . . Data!

A principal we know in a small rural school in a community of 340 folks, with 18 teachers across K–12 grades, was very keen to lead his school in an improvement effort. He realized that the staff should first study their state achievement data to understand where exactly student needs might exist. Thus, he called a meeting of the entire staff and presented the data that had recently come from the testing company that managed the state's testing program.

He spread the many pages around the tables and asked the staff to review the material and to come up with their perceptions about areas where students had performed well and where they had not. Although the principal walked hopefully around the room for some time, the staff remained passive and unengaged. Not knowing what to do, the principal thanked everyone for coming and adjourned the meeting.

A week later he decided to try again, but this time he would call the meeting for earlier in the day when the staff would "not be so tired." To his chagrin, the previous week's experience repeated itself, and the staff did not become involved in studying the data about their students, even though encouraged by the principal. "What to do now?" wondered the administrator. Ah, he thought, those great cookies that come from the bakery in the next town would enliven the study session and help the staff to focus on the data.

He dispatched his wife to purchase the delicious macadamia nut cookies, made coffee, and welcomed the staff to the "conversation about student achievement." The cookies were a tremendous success, but examining, exploring, and interrogating the data were not. What to do now?

As luck would have it, a state department of education staff person paid a visit to the principal the following day to bring information about new state policies and to have a short visit. In the course of the visit, the principal reported his disappointment about the staff not delving into the state's data as he had hoped. "Was there something wrong with the data?" he asked. Patiently and with well-concealed humor, the visitor suggested that perhaps the staff had not had professional development that would help them to understand and interpret the data. "Oh," the principal responded, "that's probably it," and he asked her, "Can you come and help us to learn how to unravel the mysteries of our data?" "Sure," she said.

The following week, without cookies, but with a well-developed plan for supporting the staff in reviewing the data, the department representative joined with the staff and led them through a lesson on reviewing their data. Toward the end of the session, as the group was examining item analysis in their content areas, the young science teacher jumped up and yelped, "Hey, look at this. I thought the kids got that concept about volume and mass . . . obviously they didn't. I'll have to teach it differently next time."

Did they "get it"? Yes, and the principal "got it" and learned that just presenting data does not guarantee that the staff can make good use of it.

Rocks in the Road

Monitoring is a time-consuming task. How do leaders make time for it? A visit to the school board to explain the benefits of the staff organized as a community of professional learners could be a realistic way to proceed. The school board members will need to understand why time is required for the staff to meet to learn together. A significant issue for the board members is to realize that the goal of the PLC is to serve students more effectively; and to do this, time is needed for staff learning and for the monitoring of staff learning. Many board members (and the public at large) assume that educators come to their jobs with everything that they will ever need to know to help students learn. In petitioning for time, this issue must be addressed, discussed, and understood. And, the wise principals tell us to protect time that has been provided; use it wisely lest it be taken away.

There is, of course, a skill in monitoring and in using the various tools that have been suggested. Thus, the principal as the initial monitor will need professional development to learn to use monitoring strategies. This is not a large boulder in the road, but an item that needs attention and should not be ignored. As teachers do not come to the classroom with the latest research-based instructional strategies, so principals learn much of their job on the job. Soliciting time and funds to gain expertise in monitoring should be an initial action for the development of the principal's role, and the district's human resources or staff development director should be a target for this request.

And, there is no way to check progress or monitor appropriately unless there is clarity about what is to be monitored. One of the most frequent failures of changing schools for improvement is lack of a clear focus or mental image of what the intended change really looks like. As discussed earlier in this chapter, a protocol or instrument, such as the Innovation Configuration Map, can be used to communicate to everyone what the new practice looks like when it is implemented in a high-quality way in classrooms or the school. This same instrument, then, can be used to check the progress of each staff member's implementation of new practices, and to assess how the PLC is being implemented by teams or the whole school community. Change process colleagues maintain that the IC provides precision to the task of monitoring.

Engage in Learning Activities

Create a small group (two or three individuals plus yourself) to discuss the issue of monitoring and to select from the following activities:

1. Visit with your district's staff development director to learn about possibilities for developing the skills of monitoring your school's implementation of new practices. If there is no director, check into your regional Comprehensive Center for help, or other external assistance providers.

2. Enroll in a workshop or other professional development activity in order to develop the knowledge and skills of monitoring or checking progress. This is most helpful if your committee (organized previously) attends with you so that you can work together, briefing and debriefing with each other as you put your new skills into operation.

3. After you have had considerable experience in monitoring the work of your school's professional learning community, invite community members to learn this skill from you and your committee of monitors so that they can help and assist each other, distributing this work across the community.

So, what did we learn from the whole experience? Could we have prepared differently? What do we wish we would have known, now that we have been through the experience? What will we share with others to help them have a better trip? What are the things that are absolutely essential to do next time? Who else would like to go? Would we be a good advertisement for this trip?

7

What Have We Learned?

If it isn't working, try something else.

High school principal

High-performing organizations are full of high-performing people.

Roland Barth

You can't do hard, thoughtful work in the fast lane. You have to slow down.

Middle school principal

In our experience, studying professional learning communities (PLCs) in schools of different sizes, different grade levels, different geographic locations, and different demographics, we have gained a few insights and lessons learned along the way. These lessons, like many new learnings, are from trial and error, application of research-based theories, and the work of committed teachers and principals who continue to do their best. Perhaps the following lessons will provide additional guidance for you when initiating and sustaining professional learning communities.

Lessons Learned

We have worked with many schools as consultants and one of us has worked as an administrator. Each school has a different set of circumstances, different strengths among the staff, and different cultures. However, this book has been about the structures, policies, and operations that hold the best chance for success across these differences.

We have learned many lessons throughout the years we have worked with schools. Most of us know by experience that whatever the plans, intended consequences sometimes happen. Unintended consequences always happen. The following are some of the bigger insights we have gained from experience.

Mandates Not Preferred

Mandates can work if principals and teachers share the same vision and are committed participants who follow through to reach their vision. Sometimes mandates are the only option—when the state department speaks, most everyone listens. However, gaining shared vision, learning, and working collaboratively, and developing shared leadership usually does not happen as a result of mandates. Professional learning communities evolve from the ongoing committed work of teachers and principals.

Think of how many mandated initiatives have begun, only to disappear after a time. Even when a program has merit, according to our experience, a mandate alone won't do it. This is one of the reasons we believe leadership is so very important. Leadership must create a positive future that allows professionals to work together. The leader must attract professionals to that preferred future. It is not enough to be dissatisfied with the current state, there has to be a desired state people want for themselves and others. This takes persistence and commitment.

Innovation *du Jour*

The tendency in our schools is to do everything for everybody. To do this we sometimes get enamored with the latest idea. We hear about something that another school has done, the latest book with a great plan of action, or we attend a workshop with a 10-step "how-to" program. We are not saying that we should ignore new thoughts. We are saying that any new approach should be a conscious choice made by the staff with a plan for implementing it and how to assess whether or not the new idea works. We don't think that schools are reticent to change; we think they attempt too many changes without full implementation and assessment.

Please don't jump from one thing to another. Many schools and districts seem to use the microwave oven approach in their school change experiences—just pop the new program in for three minutes, stir once, and it's done. Hedgehogs do not jump from idea to idea. In other words, don't abandon the process just because you don't make progress immediately. Make sure you support the staff as they move through the implementation dip—the time when staff members are trying new skills and have not incorporated the new ways into their practice. An example might be trying to use cooperative learning. At first, it is not easy and seems awkward. Eventually, as a teacher becomes more accustomed to the technique, it becomes easier.

Share the Wealth

As staff members continue to learn what works, what doesn't work, and to develop new ideas, keep in mind that sharing repertoire with the professionals creates shared wisdom throughout the school. If individual teachers are learning, help distribute the learning. Professional learning communities share learning with colleagues and the larger group. Principals and teachers must continually look for ways to learn from each other and the results of their experiences. To increase the sense of community, find ways to share the results so that the whole school learns from each individual.

In a high school where we worked, teachers were visitors in each other's classrooms. To make this possible, one strategy was hiring a substitute for the day, which can relieve four to six teachers to visit other classrooms. Two teachers talked about how in visiting their biology and English classes, they learned from each other. The biology teacher said as a result of visiting the English teachers' classes, he was now having his students journal. The English teacher said because of spending time in the biology classroom, he was now using the scientific method as a way to teach writing themes. It seems that when leaders support shared learning, good things can happen, such as instructional cross-pollination.

Critical Elements for Successful Professional Learning Community Operation

There are a number of elements so critical to effective professional learning communities that we think they are worthy of noting one more time.

Leadership and Collegial Support

Leadership and collegial support are imperative. Without leadership, there will be difficulty creating a common vision and developing shared leadership. Principals and teachers are inextricably linked. We have never seen a great principal without great staff members who contribute to leading the school. High-quality professionals deserve great leadership. We also believe that a leader must follow sometimes. One strategy we suggest is, if you think it is easy to follow, sing along in the car with others, singing back-up. We like '50s and '60s music. Try singing in the back-up role. It is much easier to sing lead and let others follow. Follow sometimes; you will be a better leader.

Collegial Learning and Collaborative Work

On many pages of this book, you have seen our words about collegial learning, which we believe to be the significant factor that distinguishes professional learning communities from other groups that meet together. For example, individuals gather at a bus stop, but we would not consider that they are a team or a community of learning professionals. It may be that they plan together to flag the bus and ensure that the bus stops at their location. In this case, we could say that the group has become a team (of sorts, albeit temporarily), for they have identified a common goal and collaborated to reach the goal. Have the individuals learned anything from this activity? Probably not, unless they have never seen a bus driver come to a screeching halt upon spying a good-looking, handsomely endowed female circled by eight other persons who are pointing toward her as she pulls her skirt up a few notches to attract his attention, so her fellow bus riders can climb aboard.

Staff can most certainly acquire information through collaboration with colleagues on grade-level teams or through whole school community meetings. But the critical point is whether they are learning what has been planned to learn. A major focus of a PLC is that the community makes a decision (based on data or other imperatives) about what they need to learn together (in community) to become more effective in their work with students, so that students learn more successfully.

The PLC's collegial learning has the following important steps:

1. Identifying an area or issue that requires staff's change of knowledge and skills

2. Deciding what to learn to gain the new knowledge and skills and how to learn it

3. Engaging in the learning

4. Applying the learning appropriately in classrooms

5. Debriefing with colleagues about "how it went" and assessing effectiveness

6. Revising, based on the new learning from experience, and applying again

One could say that collegial learning should be intentional learning, agreed upon by the colleagues and based on a common goal or need. Many organizations claim to be professional learning communities and describe themselves as doing collaborative work. We wonder if they ever get to the middle word in the PLC label and engage in learning that will increase and enhance the professionals' knowledge, skills, and effectiveness.

Professional Teams Vis-à-Vis Whole School Professional Communities

Many schools claim to be a PLC and point to their grade-level teams or academic discipline teams that meet regularly for planning and collaborative work. We believe these structures are important, as they provide teachers the opportunity to focus on the particular needs of their grade or subject matter students. Meeting together is a positive step. The important element in a PLC centers around *what* are we doing when we meet. As Figure 3.1 suggested, when the school is organized in subgroup teams with no overarching whole school structure to do community learning and development, there is a lack of a unified purpose and the small groups lack the opportunity to converge with a common goal. When the whole school is committed to the shared vision of staff member learning, everyone participates. The message to our staff members and the public is clear: learning is our school's goal.

Good Shepherd Versus Bo Peep

There is a practice in leadership we refer to as the "Bo Peep" style of leadership. This is where you leave staff members alone and assume they will follow through, following behind the leader. We do not think that works, nor will it ever work. Bo Peep management is abdication. However, we emphatically support the "Good Shepherd" theory. This theory-in-action is tending to the professionals in the building. You do this by keeping the flock together in order to reach a destination with minimal interruptions. A good shepherd also watches out for the staff, similar to servant leadership. A good shepherd becomes part of the flock and is not separated from the group. The good shepherd watches over the flock, protecting them from wolves, makes sure there is food in the meadows to eat, and makes sure no one gets separated from the flock.

Servant leadership was proposed by Robert Greenleaf (1977), who suggested that a leader must serve those he or she is leading. A principal we know has a paper clip theory. He says if bringing a box of paper clips to a room will help a teacher teach better and students learn better, he is on his way with the box. Leadership cannot make professional learning communities happen alone. Shared leadership, staff learning, trust, and collaboration are the factors that will create and sustain a PLC and the culture needed to increase student learning.

Focus and Communication

The leader communicates, communicates, and communicates with the staff and the school's constituency that learning is the school's business, the school's product, and the school's process. Once the course is set, the leader communicates on a regular basis. Staff members forget when other pressing issues take conscious attention and time. This is when it is critical for the leader to communicate the focus on learning. The need to keep focus and attention will never go away. Take professional learning communities for granted and they will change into something different. To use Collins' (2001) tenet, be a hedgehog, stay on message.

Vignettes

Implementing a Mandate:
The Right Way to Get Started

There are times when mandates must be implemented: "Right-to-Know" for hazardous chemicals, state testing, and child endangerment mandates, to name a few. However, in several schools we know, mandates can harden the cynics and divert time and energy when staff members discuss whether or not they will comply. One school tried Writing Across the Curriculum. The research was clear about the impact on student writing. There were some teachers who did not want to change their styles of teaching or the content they covered.

The administrator and teacher leaders who supported the writing program began the implementation by hosting meetings to find out the concerns of the staff who did not want to incorporate the new strategies. Most of the time, if staff feel they are listened to, they will support the initiative at some level.

Initiative *du Jour*

A principal in an inner-city school was hired to change the culture for the better. The supervisor of the principal wanted to know the goals for the upcoming school year. The principal fell into the trap of wanting to please and solve every issue quickly. The principal provided eight goals to the assistant superintendent for the school year. By midyear, the principal knew that he would be lucky to achieve three out of the eight. At the end of the year, he could only point to evidence of three goals being addressed. One was completed; there was increased trust among the teaching staff and the administration.

Another goal of developing teacher leadership was well on its way to making major shifts with operating the school, and a third, building cleanliness with the custodial staff, was about half-successful. The other five goals were barely worked on during the year.

In the conference at the end of the year, the assistant superintendent reviewed the eight goals with the principal. At the end of the conference, the assistant superintendent asked the principal to declare goals for next year. The principal explained that he would take four of the eight goals from last year. The assistant superintendent thought the principal should come up with new goals. The principal stated that he would stay with half of what he started, to stay with some of the original goals to make it work better, and he would reduce the goals to four.

The principal also said, putting out new goals would keep everyone trying to change new things rather than getting better results with trust, leadership, and building issues. To divert our attention to other goals would lead to backsliding.

Share the Wealth

In an urban elementary school, the test scores had been very low for a number of years. A new principal took over, and within three months noticed that there were a number of great teachers working very well with students. She wondered why some of the teachers were doing well with the same kids that others were having difficulty with in the same school.

As she observed classes, she found that there were some genuine star teachers in the school, even though the school had a bad reputation for test scores. She initiated a program of "Positive Deviance," based on the work of Jerry Sternin (2002), to find out what was working. Once strategies and processes were identified, the principal then held meetings called "Strategy Marts." Teachers started meeting to share what was working. This shared ideas among the school.

As assistant superintendent picked up the idea and held the same kind of process in an area of the city that had multiple low test scores in several buildings. The repertoire continued to be shared among staff members, and test scores started to increase.

Rocks in the Road

There are numerous externally driven intrusions that can interrupt the school's work. Be ready to bar the door.

Protection

The leader protects the staff members and holds the time for professional learning communities sacred. There will be many inquiries and invitations for leaders to have meetings: on new programs, insurance and retirement companies that want to address the staff, and well-intentioned community members who have heard of great new ideas that the school should implement. Of course, there may be merit to some of these resources coming from outside the school. However, the question is always, "How does this new idea help students learn better?" "How will this new program assist our staff in building a collaborative learning culture?" "What will we have to give up in order to begin a new initiative?" Protecting the staff from outside distractions can be a full-time job. It is a leadership role.

Protecting the staff is also necessary from an internal perspective. Sometimes the district or the system has too many initiatives or changes occurring at one time. We know from change literature that an organization can only attend to a few changes at a time. Overstimulation can lead to fragmentation, exhaustion, and poor results. Keep the focus on learning and lead courageous conversations within the district. Occasionally a district need may interfere with your professional learning community. One principal we know had to tell the superintendent that professional learning communities were more important than the superintendent's message to the staff. This was not an easy conversation. It did send the message of the importance of learning at this school.

Political Winds

"There be dragons." This is what old mapmakers used to write in areas where they did not know what was there. In our current educational state there are dragons lurking. There are community members who just wait for something not to work and then pounce on the school. Some of these outside the community think identifying what is wrong is enough to change the system or to intimidate people to change the system. We think honest criticism is helpful, and we invite constituents to bring a suggestion. This is why data are so important. The question is, "How do we know we are getting better, getting worse or staying the same?" Conduct midyear assessments. Reflect on the process. Make necessary changes for the benefit of the staff members. Let staff members lead. Staff members, armed with results, can be a powerful force for school improvement.

Our Final Message

And, now, a few last reminders.

Courage

Murphy (2006) has suggested that principals take an ethical stand while putting on the learning lens, focusing on students and what they are learning, rather than be seduced by the organizational routines that sometimes get in the way of learning. Principals will have to demonstrate great courage to help focus schools on learning and not be driven by political agendas, personal desires of individual constituents, and taking personal attacks on their credibility.

A principal we know uses a Native American metaphor for courage. He calls it a "suicide spear." It is where you put your spear in the ground that says, "This is where I will stand. If you are going to kill me, kill me on this issue, right here." So, we ask you, "What are you willing to take a stand for?" "What will you go to the wall for?" "What will it take to make learning the number one priority in your school?"

Commitment

As we mentioned before, there is a different commitment between the chicken and the pig when making bacon and eggs. However, we need both to make the final product. We offer some questions for you to consider. Please do not take these questions lightly, for this is not for the faint of heart.

- Do you really believe that professional learning communities can make a difference for staff members and ultimately result in increased student learning?
- Are you committed to persevering to change current practices to those that increase effectiveness? Can you stay on message?
- Do you have the patience to make mistakes, share leadership, and commit time for reflection? Are you committed to progress, not perfection?
- Does your walk match your talk? Most people like to hear the words but will watch the walk to determine the sincerity of the message. People will judge your authenticity by the distance between what you say and what you do.

Collegiality

The National Center for Educational Statistics (2004), "Teacher Mobility and Attrition," describes teacher turnover rates. In Texas, 40 percent, and nationwide, 50 percent, of the teachers leave the profession in the first five years. These rates are higher in urban areas, where the highest number of low-performing schools exist. Some schools with a high percentage of poverty have rates at 80 percent turnover. Two of the top reasons for leaving are dissatisfaction with support from administrators and dissatisfaction with workplace conditions. We believe professional learning communities are an excellent way to provide the support, collegiality, intellectual stimulation, and feedback for our less experienced teachers. The connectedness that grows out of studying, learning and finding new ways to be effective will provide meaning for themselves personally and make a difference professionally.

We believe that without addressing workplace conditions, the trend of high attrition will continue. Specifically, we think organizations must focus on mutual support and respect, give attention to how we bring new teachers into the system, provide mentors and provide coaches, and make schools intellectually stimulating for the adults, so they can continue to grow and learn. In Weisbord (1987),

Fred Emery details six intrinsic motivational factors that make work satisfying. They are

1. Variety and challenge

2. Elbow room for decision making

3. Feedback and learning

4. Mutual support and respect

5. Wholeness and meaning

6. Room to grow—a bright future

This would be a great place to start to create the conditions that will attract and retain those people who want to be teachers and principals.

Knowing-Doing Gap

We ask again, can we close the knowing-doing gap? We know what to do in order to produce higher results. Can we make the choices necessary to behave in alignment with what we know is best for staff members, principals and students? The hard facts are that this takes courage, commitment, and collegiality.

Closing the knowing-doing gap requires time to talk, a process of reflection to learn from our professional practices, and constant monitoring of actual results with intended results. Without changing practice, teachers and principals will continue to show up at school, put in tremendous amounts of efforts to deal with a changing environment, and probably show modest increases in results. As comedian Moms Mabley once said, "If you always do what you did, you always get what you got."

Reflection

There have been many authors in business and education—Chris Argyris, Donald Schön, Jerome Kagan, and Stephen Brookfield, to name a few—who have promoted reflection to increase organizational learning. In York-Barr, Sommers, Ghere, and Montie (2006), there are many examples of reflective practice to increase staff member learning and student achievement. As important as reflection is, this may be the most difficult to implement. Reflection takes time, and time is our most important nonrenewable resource.

A principal once said, "If we can't figure out a way to reflect on our practice, we won't make substantive progress." We believe that learning together requires conversations and reflection. We strongly advocate for reflection to be part of any professional learning community. Taking time to reflect has a cost. Not taking time to reflect has a bigger cost in terms of learning.

Trust

Develop trust, for it will pay huge dividends. As professional learning communities become embedded into the culture of school, trust increases. Spending time with other teachers on common challenges builds familiarity, understanding of diverse perspectives, and working together toward solutions. More time will be devoted to learning and less to self-protection. Creating high-trust cultures in schools means the adults openly, without hesitation, will ask for *and* receive help. As W. Edwards Deming said years ago, "Drive out fear." These words are still as important today as they were in the middle of the Total Quality Management heyday. With trust people will reach out, not fearing they will look inadequate or that they will be ridiculed.

Tschannen-Moran (2004) declares, "Without the confidence that a person's words can be relied upon and can accurately predict future actions, trust is unlikely to develop" (p. 22). She goes on to describe three elements of behavior that encourage and enhance trust. First, accept accountability. Principals and teachers must accept responsibility and are willing to be held accountable. Second, avoid manipulation that will undermine trust. We all know when we are being manipulated and we will not open ourselves to people who behave that way. And, third, be real; we all have a role to play. Even though our roles as principals may require making unpopular decisions, we can still be a "real person." Tschannen-Moran concludes, "One of a principal's primary responsibilities is to protect the core work of the school—the teaching and learning process" (p. 32). We think that is a sound core value, and at the heart of the leader's role in a PLC school.

References

Amason, A., Thompson, K., Hochwarter, W., & Harrison, A. (1995, August). Conflict: An important dimension in successful management teams. *Organizational Dynamics*, 20–35.

Argyris, C. (1990). *Overcoming organizational defenses.* New York: Prentice Hall.

Argyris, C., & Schön, D. (1978). *Organizational learning.* Reading, MA: Addison-Wesley.

Bandura, A. (1997). *Self efficacy.* New York: Worth Publishing.

Barth, R. (1990). *Improving schools from within: Teachers, parents, and principals can make the difference.* San Francisco: Jossey-Bass.

Barth, R. (2006, March). Improving relationships within the schoolhouse. *Educational Leadership, 63*(6), 8–13.

Bateson, M. C. (1989). *Composing a life.* New York: Atlantic Monthly Press.

Beckhard, R. (1987). *Organizational transitions.* Reading, MA: Addison-Wesley.

Bennis, W. (1989). *Why leaders can't lead.* San Francisco: Jossey-Bass.

Block, P. (2003). *The answer to how is yes.* San Francisco: Berrett-Koehler.

Bobbett, J. J., Ellett, C. D., Teddlie, C., Olivier, D. F., & Rugutt, J. (2002, April). *School culture and school effectiveness in demonstrably effective and ineffective schools.* Paper presented at the annual meeting of the American Education Research Association, New Orleans.

Bohm, D. (1989). *On dialogue.* Notes from seminar on November 6, Ojai, CA.

Boyd, V. (1992). *School context: Bridge or barrier to school change?* Austin, TX: Southwest Educational Development Laboratory.

Brandt, R. (1995). On restructuring schools: A conversation with Fred Newmann. *Educational Leadership, 53*(3), 70–73.

Bryk, A. S., & Schneider, B. (2002). *Trust in schools: A core resource for improvement.* New York: Russell Sage Foundation.

Burley-Allen, M. (1995). *The forgotten art of listening.* New York: Wiley.

Carse, J. (1986). *Finite and infinite games.* New York: Ballantine Books.

Chadwick, B. (1995). *Conflict to consensus workshop.* Minneapolis, MN: Minneapolis Public Schools.

Collins, J. (2001). *Good to great.* New York: HarperCollins.

Collins, J. (2005). *Good to great and the social sector: A monograph to accompany Good to Great.* Boulder, CO: Author.

Cooper, R., & Sawaf, A. (1996). *Executive EQ.* New York: Grosset/Putnam.

Costa, A., & Garmston, R. (2002). *The art of cognitive coaching: A foundation for renaissance schools.* Norwood, MA: Christopher-Gordon.

Covey, S. (1989). *The 7 habits of highly effective people.* New York: Simon & Schuster.

Deal, T. E., & Peterson, K. D. (1990). *The principal's role in shaping school culture.* Washington, DC: U.S. Department of Education.

Deci, E. (1995). *Why we do what we do.* New York: Grosset Putnam.

Doyle, M., & Straus, D. (1976). *How to make meetings work.* New York: Berkley Publishing Group.

Edmonds, R. (1979, October). Effective schools for the urban poor. *Educational Leadership, 37*(1), 15–24.

Farson, R. (1996). *Management of the absurd.* New York: Touchstone.

Farson, R., & Keyes, R. (2002). *Whoever makes the most mistakes wins.* New York: Free Press.

Fullan, M. (2001). *Leading in a culture of change.* San Francisco: Jossey-Bass.

Fullan, M., & Hargreaves, A. (1996). *What's worth fighting for in your school?* New York: Teachers College Press.

Garmston, R., & Wellman, B. (1999). *Adaptive schools.* Norwood, MA: Christopher-Gordon.

Garreau, Joel. (2005). *Radical evolution.* New York: Random House.

George, A. A., Hall, G. E., & Stiegelbauer, S. M. (2006). *Measuring implementation in schools: The Stages of Concern Questionnaire.* Austin, TX: Southwest Educational Development Laboratory.

Gonzalez, C. E., Resta, P. E., & De Hoyos, M. L. (2005, April). *Barriers and facilitators on implementation of policy initiatives to transform higher education teaching-learning process.* Paper presented at the annual meeting of the American Educational Research Association, Seattle.

Greenleaf, R. (1977). *Servant leadership.* Mahwah, NJ: Paulist Press.

Hall, G. E., Dirksen, D. J., & George, A. A. (2006). *Measuring implementation in schools: Levels of use.* Austin, TX: Southwest Educational Development Laboratory.

Hall, G. E., & Hord, S. M. (2006). *Implementing change: Patterns, principles, and potholes.* Boston: Allyn & Bacon.

Hall, G. E., Hord, S. M., George, A. A., Stiegelbauer, S. M., & Dirksen, D. (2006). *Implementing change in schools: The Concerns-Based Adoption Model.* Austin, TX: Southwest Educational Development Laboratory.

Hall, G. E., Wallace, R. C., & Dossett, W. A. (1973). *A developmental conceptualization of the adoption process within educational institutions.* ERIC Document Reproduction Service No. ED 095 126.

Hargreaves, A. (2003). *Teaching in the knowledge society: Education in the age of insecurity.* New York: Teachers College Press.

Hargreaves, A., & Fink, D. (2006). *Sustainable leadership.* San Francisco: Jossey-Bass.

Harris, M. (1968). *The rise of anthropological theory.* New York: Crowell.

Harvey, T., & Drolet, B. (2004). *Building teams, building people.* Lanham, MD: Rowman & Littlefield.

Herbert, K. S., Murphy, K. M., Ramos, M. A., Vaden-Kiernan, M., & Buttram, J. L. (2006). *SEDL's Working Systemically Model final report.* Austin, TX: Southwest Educational Development Laboratory.

Hord, S. M. (2000a). Assessing a school staff as a community of professional learners. *Issues About Change, 7*(1). Retrieved September 6, 2007, from http://www.sedl.org/change/issues/issues71/

Hord, S. M. (2000b). Change is learning: It's as simple and complicated as that. *Journal of Classroom Interaction, 35*(1), 26–27.

Hord, S. M. (Ed.). (2004). *Learning together, leading together: Changing schools through professional learning communities.* New York: Teachers College Press.

Hord, S. M., & Rutherford, W. L. (1998). Creating a professional learning community: Cottonwood Creek School. *Issues About Change, 6*(2).

Hord, S. M., Rutherford, W. L., Huling-Austin, L. L., & Hall, G. E. (2004). *Taking charge of change.* Alexandria, VA: Association for Supervision and Curriculum Development.

Hord, S. M., Stiegelbauer, S. M., Hall, G. E., & George, A. A. (2006). *Measuring implementation in schools: Innovation configurations.* Austin, TX: Southwest Educational Development.

Hunter, M. (1976, April). Teacher competency: Problem, theory, and practice. *Theory Into Practice, 15*(2), 162–171.

Intrator, S. M., & Kunzman, R. (2006, March). Starting with the soul. *Educational Leadership, 63*(6), 38–42.

Isaacs, W. (1999). *Dialogue: The art of thinking together.* New York: Currency.

Jolly, A. (2005). *A facilitator's guide to professional learning teams.* Greensboro, NC: SERVE.

Joyce, B., & Showers, B. (1988). *Student achievement through staff development.* New York: Longman.

Joyce, B., & Showers, B. (2002). *Student achievement through staff development.* (3rd ed.). Alexandria, VA: Association for Supervision and Curriculum Development.

Killion, J. (2002). *Assessing impact: Evaluating staff development.* Oxford, OH: National Staff Development Council.

Klein, G. (1998). *Sources of power: How people make decisions.* Cambridge, MA: MIT Press.

Kleine-Kracht, P. A. (1993). The principal in a community of learning. *Journal of School Leadership, 3*(4), 391–399.

Kohn, A. (1993). *Punished by rewards: The trouble with gold stars, incentive plans, A's, praise, and other bribes.* New York: Houghton Mifflin.

Lambert, L. (1998). *Building leadership capacity in schools.* Alexandria, VA: Association for Supervision and Curriculum Development.

Lee, V. E., Smith, J. B., & Croninger, R. G. (1995, Fall). Another look at high school restructuring. *Issues in restructuring schools.* Madison: University of Wisconsin-Madison, School of Education, Center on Organization and Restructuring Schools.

Leithwood, K., & Jantzi, D. (1990). *Transformational leadership: How principals can help reform school culture.* Paper presented at American Educational Research Association annual meeting.

Leithwood, K., Seashore-Louis, K., Anderson, S., & Wahlstrom, K. (2004). *How leadership influences student learning.* Minneapolis: University of Minnesota, Center for Applied Research and Educational Improvement; Toronto: University of Toronto, Ontario Institute for Studies in Education.

Retrieved June 28, 2007, from http://education.umn.edu/CAREI/leadership/ReviewofResearch.pdf

Lippitt, M. (2003). *Leading complex change.* Potomac, MD: Enterprise Management.

Louis, K. S., & Kruse, S. D. (1995). *Professionalism and community: Perspectives on reforming urban schools.* Thousand Oaks, CA: Corwin Press.

Machiavelli, N. (1532/1908). *The prince* (W. K. Marriott, Trans.). Retrieved June 27, 2007, from http://www.gutenberg.org/files/1232/1232.txt

Marzano, R. J., Waters, T., & McNulty, B. A. (2005). *School leadership that works: From research to results.* Alexandria, VA: Association for Supervision and Curriculum Development.

McLaughlin, L., & Hyle, A. E. (2001, April). *The school principal as change agent: An exploratory case study.* Paper presented at the annual meeting of the American Educational Research Association, Seattle, WA.

McLaughlin, M., & Phillips, D. (Eds.). (1991). *Evaluation and education: A quarter century.* Chicago: University of Chicago Press.

McLaughlin, M. W., & Talbert, J. E. (2006). *Building school-based teacher learning communities: Professional strategies to improve student achievement.* New York: Teachers College Press.

McLean, W. R., & Toler-Robinson, E. (2001, Spring). Building urban educational partnerships. *Journal of School Improvement, 2*(1), 39–42.

Meehan, M. L., Orletsky, S. R., & Sattes, B. (1997). *Field test of an instrument measuring the concepts of professional learning communities in schools.* Charleston, WV: Appalachia Educational Laboratory. (ERIC Document Reproduction Service No. ED433358). Retrieved April 30, 2007, from the ERIC database.

Morrell, M., & Capparell, S. (2001). *Shackleton's way: Leadership lessons from the great Antarctic explorer.* New York: Penguin Putnam.

Murphy, C. U., & Lick, D. W. (2005). *Whole-faculty study groups* (3rd ed.). Thousand Oaks, CA: Corwin Press.

Murphy, J. (2006). A new view of leadership. *Journal of Staff Development, 27*(3), 51–52, 64.

National Center for Educational Statistics. (2004). *Teacher mobility and attrition: Results from the teacher follow-up survey, 2000–2001.* Washington, DC: U.S. Department of Education, Institute of Education Sciences. Retrieved on July 5, 2007, from http://nces.ed.gov/pubsearch/pubsinfo.asp?pubid=2004301

Naylor, C. 2005. *A teacher union's collaborative research agenda and strategies: One way forward for Canadian teacher unions in supporting teacher's professional development?* Vancouver, BC: British Columbia Teachers Federation Research Report 2005-TR-01. Retrieved October 22, 2007, from http://www.bctf.ca/publications/ResearchReports.aspx?id=9116.

O'Hanlon, B. (1999). *Do one thing different.* New York: Morrow.

Olsen, W. R., & Sommers, W. A. (2004). *A trainer's companion: Stories to stimulate reflection, conversation, action.* Thousand Oaks, CA: Corwin Press.

Palmer, P. (1998). *The courage to teach.* San Francisco: Jossey-Bass.

Perkins, D. (2003). *King Arthur's round table: How collaborative conversations create smart organizations.* Hoboken, NJ: Wiley.

Peters, T. (2003). *Re-Imagine*. London: Dorling Kindersley.

Pfeffer, J., & Sutton, R. I. (2000). *The knowing-doing gap: How smart companies turn knowledge into action*. Boston: Harvard Business School Press.

Rosenholtz, S. J. (1989). *Teachers' workplace*. New York: Longman.

Roy, P., & Hord, S. (2003). *Moving NSDC's staff development standards into practice: Innovation configurations*. Oxford, OH: National Staff Development Council.

Rust, F. O., & Freidus, H. (2001). *Guiding school change: The role and work of change agents*. New York: Teachers College Press.

Sarason, S. B. (1990). *The predictable failure of education reform: Can we change course before it is too late?* San Francisco: Jossey-Bass.

Schein, E. (1992). *Organizational culture and leadership: A dynamic view* (2nd ed.). San Francisco: Jossey-Bass.

Schlechty, P. (1993, Fall). On the frontier of school reform with trailblazers, pioneers, and settlers. *Journal of Staff Development, 14*(4), 46–51.

Schön, D. (1983). *The reflective practitioner*. New York: Basic Books.

Scott, S. (2002). *Fierce conversations*. New York: Penguin Putnam.

Senge, P. (1990). *The fifth discipline*. New York: Doubleday Current.

Sommers, W., & Payne, R. (2001). *Living on a tightrope: A survival handbook for principals*. Baytown, TX: AhaProcess.

Sparks, D. (2005). *Leading for results*. Thousand Oaks, CA: Corwin Press.

Spillane, J. (2006). *Distributed leadership*. San Francisco: Jossey-Bass.

Spradley, J. P. (1979). *The ethnographic review*. New York: Holt, Rinehart & Winston.

Sternin, J. (2002). Positive deviance: A new paradigm for addressing today's problems today. *Journal of Corporate Citizenship, 5*, 57–62.

Straus, D. (2002). *How to make collaboration work*. San Francisco: Berrett-Koehler.

Tichy, N. (1997). *The leadership engine*. New York: HarperCollins.

Tschannen-Moran, M. (2004). *Trust matters: Leadership for successful schools*. San Francisco: Jossey-Bass.

Vygotsky. L. (1986). *Thought and language*. Cambridge, MA: MIT Press.

Waters, T., & Kingston, S. (2005, September/October). The standards we need. *Leadership, 35*(1), 14–16, 36–39.

Weisbord, M. (1987). *Productive workplaces*. San Francisco: Jossey-Bass.

Wenger, E. (1998). *Communities of practice*. Cambridge, UK: Cambridge University Press.

Wheatley, M., & Kellner-Rogers, M. (1996). *A simpler way*. San Francisco: Berrett-Koehler.

Wignall, R. (1992, June). *Building a collaborative school culture: A case study of one woman in the principalship*. Paper presented at the European Conference on Educational Research, Enschede, The Netherlands.

Wilson, E. (1999). *The diversity of life*. New York: Norton.

Wolfe, P. (2001). *Brain matters*. Alexandria, VA: Association of Supervision and Curriculum Development.

York-Barr, J., Sommers, W., Ghere, G., & Montie, J. (2006). *Reflective practice to improve schools* (2nd ed.). Thousand Oaks, CA: Corwin Press.

Zander, B., & Zander, R. (2000). *The art of possibility*. Boston: Harvard Business School Press.

Index

CORWIN PRESS

The Corwin Press logo—a raven striding across an open book—represents the union of courage and learning. Corwin Press is committed to improving education for all learners by publishing books and other professional development resources for those serving the field of PreK–12 education. By providing practical, hands-on materials, Corwin Press continues to carry out the promise of its motto: **"Helping Educators Do Their Work Better."**

NATIONAL ASSOCIATION OF SECONDARY SCHOOL PRINCIPALS

Promoting Excellence in School Leadership

The National Association of Secondary School Principals—promoting excellence in school leadership since 1916—provides its members the professional resources to serve as visionary leaders. NASSP further promotes student leadership development through its sponsorship of the National Honor Society®, the National Junior Honor Society®, and the National Association of Student Councils®. For more information, visit www.principals.org.

NSDC's mission is to ensure success for all students by serving as the international network for those who improve schools and by advancing individual and organization development.